CONFUCIANISM
AND
AMERICAN
PHILOSOPHY

SUNY series in Chinese Philosophy and Culture
Roger T. Ames, editor

CONFUCIANISM AND AMERICAN PHILOSOPHY

Mathew A. Foust

Cover image: Thoreau's journal entry from his Commonplace Book (1830-1862) is from the Berg Collection of the New York Public Library archives/digital collections.

Published by State University of New York Press, Albany

© 2017 State University of New York

All rights reserved

Printed in the United States of America

No part of this book may be used or reproduced in any manner whatsoever without written permission. No part of this book may be stored in a retrieval system or transmitted in any form or by any means including electronic, electrostatic, magnetic tape, mechanical, photocopying, recording, or otherwise without the prior permission in writing of the publisher.

For information, contact State University of New York Press, Albany, NY
www.sunypress.edu

Production, Diane Ganeles
Marketing, Anne M. Valentine

Library of Congress Cataloging-in-Publication Data

Names: Foust, Mathew A., author.
Title: Confucianism and American philosophy / by Mathew A. Foust.
Description: Albany, NY : State University of New York, 2017. | Series: SUNY series in Chinese philosophy and culture | Includes bibliographical references and index.
Identifiers: LCCN 2016031491 (print) | LCCN 2017004917 (ebook) | ISBN 9781438464756 (hardcover : alk. paper) | ISBN 978-1-4384-6474-9 (paperback : alk. paper) | ISBN 9781438464763 (e-book)
Subjects: LCSH: Philosophy, Confucian—China. | Confucianism—China. | Philosophy, American.
Classification: LCC B127.C65 F68 2017 (print) | LCC B127.C65 (ebook) | DDC 181/.112—dc23
LC record available at https://lccn.loc.gov/2016031491

10 9 8 7 6 5 4 3 2 1

To my friends in China

Contents

ACKNOWLEDGMENTS	xi
INTRODUCTION	1
On Comparative Philosophy	1
American Philosophy as World Philosophy	5
Confucius and Dewey	7
Broadening a Comparative Horizon	10
Boston Confucianism	11
Textual Conventions	12
Overview	14
1. CONFUCIANISM AND EMERSON: FRIENDSHIP	19
Introduction	19
"Have no friend unlike yourself"	22
Confucian Friendship	25
Confucianism in Emerson's "Friendship"	32
Conclusion	39
2. CONFUCIANISM AND THOREAU: CIVIL DISOBEDIENCE	41
Introduction	41
Analects 8.13 and *Mencius* 4A5	42

On Civil Disobedience	44
Confucianism in "Civil Disobedience"	45
On Confucian Civil Disobedience	52
Conclusion	58

3. CONFUCIANISM AND PEIRCE:
   INQUIRY AND BELIEF — 61
   - Introduction — 61
   - Doubt, Inquiry, and Belief — 62
   - Peirce's Four Methods of Belief Fixation — 64
   - Confucius and the Method of Tenacity — 69
   - Confucius and the Method of Authority — 70
   - Confucius and the *A Priori* Method — 74
   - Confucius and the Scientific Method — 76
   - Conclusion — 79

4. CONFUCIANISM AND JAMES:
   HUMAN NATURE AND MORALITY — 83
   - Introduction — 83
   - Mencius and Xunzi on Human Nature and Morality — 84
   - James on Human Nature and Morality — 92
   - The Healthy-Minded and the Sick-Souled — 93
   - Human Nature, Violence, and Peace — 95
   - Conclusion — 98

5. CONFUCIANISM AND ROYCE:
   SHAME AND ATONEMENT — 101
   - Introduction — 101
   - Shame in the Thought of Royce — 104
   - Shame in the Thought of Confucius and Mencius — 108
   - Theories of Atonement — 113
   - Atonement in the Thought of Royce — 113
   - Atonement in the Thought of Confucius — 116
   - Conclusion — 126

CONCLUSION	129
Looking Back	129
Looking Ahead	131
NOTES	135
BIBLIOGRAPHY	165
INDEX	177

Acknowledgments

As an American who has lived and taught in China, I have drawn significant inspiration in writing this book from my friends on the opposite side of the globe. Many are the lasting memories that I cherish from my year at BNU-HKBU United International College in Zhuhai (2010–2011), my first full-time teaching position. The students to whom I am indebted are numerous; were I to list them, I am certain that I would commit several errors of omission. I have learned something from all of them, however, perhaps far more than I ever could have taught them. Two people who were affiliated with UIC warrant special mention: Sandra He and Genie Cui. Sandra and Genie were indefatigable and indispensable in roles as various as department administrator, teaching assistant, and cultural broker. Their patience in helping me to bridge gaps between my life in America and my life in China was essential to my sustenance in Zhuhai, and it has served as inspiration in the years since I was privileged enough to have them as my colleagues.

I have benefited from the support and counsel of several people throughout the development of this book. I am especially grateful to Roger Ames, whose encouragement at a critical time in my life as a graduate student assured me that I had ideas worth pursuing and contributing to the world of comparative philosophy. Since then, Roger has generously invested time and energy on my behalf whenever I have requested his favor to do so. Although I have never formally been Roger's student, I have learned very much from his example.

I am grateful to Chung-ying Cheng and Linyu Gu, colleagues via the *Journal of Chinese Philosophy*. Their unflagging support over the past several years has been a calming presence in the midst of the vicissitudes of academic life. I am also grateful to Sor-hoon Tan, Robert Neville, and the late Joseph Grange. Each has encouraged me during the development of this project, and their scholarship has been greatly influential.

Several friends and colleagues provided helpful feedback on preliminary versions of one or more of the chapters of this book or contributed constructive insights in conversation: Stephen C. Angle, Cameron Brewer, Susan Burdelski, Tim Connolly, David Elstein, Thorian Harris, Christopher Kirby, Andrew Komasinski, Andrew Lambert, Sydney Morrow, On-cho Ng, Ann A. Pang-White, Thomas Radice, Brian Skelly, Matt Stefon, Ian Sullivan, Winnie Sung, and Xiaomei Yang. This book is substantially better thanks to their questions and comments.

Membership in a number of professional organizations has also enabled me to receive helpful feedback on research related to this book: American Philosophical Association (APA), International Society for Chinese Philosophy (ISCP), International Society for Comparative Studies of Chinese and Western Philosophy (ISCWP), Society for the Advancement of American Philosophy (SAAP), and Society for Asian and Comparative Philosophy (SACP).

I am also indebted to the sedulous staff of SUNY Press: Christopher Ahn, Cathleen Collins, Dana Foote, Diane Ganeles, Andrew Kenyon, Jessica Kirschner, James Peltz, Anne Valentine, and the late Nancy Ellegate. Each played a vital role in seeing this project to fruition.

Preliminary versions of chapters were presented in the following forums:

> Chapter 1: "Have No Friend Unlike Yourself: Emerson's Confucian Notion of Friendship," SACP Invited Panel, Forty-Third Annual Meeting of SAAP, Portland, OR, March 3–5, 2016.

Chapter 2: "Confucius, Thoreau, and Civil Disobedience," ISCWP Session, APA-Eastern Meeting, Baltimore, MD, December 27–30, 2013.

Chapter 2: "Confucianism in Thoreau's *Civil Disobedience*," An International Conference on Hermeneutics East and West, The Pennsylvania State University, University Park, PA, May 16–17, 2014.

Chapter 2: "Emerson and Thoreau: American Confucians?," University of Hartford Philosophy Club, March 26, 2015.

Chapter 2: "Chinese Thought in American Context: Confucianism in American Transcendentalism," 2015 International Conference on Asian Studies, University of Scranton, Scranton, PA, March 28–29, 2015.

Chapter 3: "Confucius, Peirce, and the Fixation of Belief," The Charles S. Peirce International Centennial Congress, Lowell, MA, July 16–19, 2014.

Chapter 3: "Confucius and Peirce on Inquiry and Belief," ISCP Session, APA-Pacific Meeting, Vancouver, BC, Canada, April 1–4, 2015.

Chapter 5: "Time to Change: Atonement in the Philosophies of Confucius and Josiah Royce," International Society for the Study of Time Conference, "Time and Change in China and the West," Beijing Normal University, Beijing, China, June 20–22, 2014.

Chapter 5: "Making Amends with Confucius and Royce," ISCWP Session, APA-Pacific Meeting, Vancouver, BC, Canada, April 1–4, 2015.

Chapter 5: "Wrongdoing, Shame, and Atonement," University of Hartford Philosophy Club, October 15, 2015.

Chapter 5: "Atonement in the *Analects*," 2015 Northeast Conference on Chinese Thought, Southern Connecticut State University, New Haven, CT, November 7–8, 2015.

Portions of the introduction and conclusion appeared in "Confucianism and American Pragmatism," *Philosophy Compass* 10, no. 6 (2015): 369–378. Portions of chapter 5 appeared in "Confess Your

Contradictions: Schelling, Royce, and the Art of Atonement," *Journal of Speculative Philosophy* 26, no. 3 (2012): 516–530.

The research related to this book was supported in part by the College of Liberal Arts and Social Sciences at Central Connecticut State University, which awarded me Research Reassigned Time during the fall 2014 and spring 2015 semesters. Research related to this book was also supported in part by a Hyundai Motor Corporation Endowment Grant via the Center for International Education at Central Connecticut State University and a Confucius China Studies Program International Conference Grant via the Confucius Institute at Central Connecticut State University, both awarded in summer 2014.

Introduction

ON COMPARATIVE PHILOSOPHY

This book is a work of comparative philosophy. In its pages are a number of comparative analyses of Confucianism and American philosophy. Before embarking on these analyses in earnest, it would be fruitful to reflect upon the nature of this enterprise. What is comparative philosophy? Is it simply the practice of comparing two or more philosophies? What is to be gained from this type of comparison? What approach to comparative philosophy is most conducive to attaining whatever gains might be had?

At first sight, it would seem that comparative philosophy is simply the practice of comparing two or more philosophies. To define comparative philosophy in this way, however, would neglect a crucial element. The following definition, from Robert W. Smid, highlights the important distinguishing feature: "Comparative philosophy can be defined by its attempt to move across boundaries of otherwise distinct philosophical traditions—especially insofar as these traditions are divided by significant historical and cultural distance—thus enabling a comparison of what lies on either side of the boundary."[1] Smid foregrounds a core component of comparative philosophy—comparative philosophy attempts to move across boundaries of otherwise distinct philosophical traditions. Moving across boundaries of otherwise distinct philosophical *traditions* is different than moving across boundaries of otherwise distinct philosophical *positions*. Consequently, a comparison of the positions of two philosophers who disagree about something is not necessarily an instance of comparative philosophy. It is essential that the comparison involve philosophers representing distinct traditions. This conception of comparative philosophy admits of some fluidity, as the notion of a "tradition" is itself fluid. For Smid, the notion of a "tradition" is better regarded as a practical designation rather than a metaphysical one, "intended to designate . . . that something *distinctive* and *of particular importance* has been passed on from one person or group to another."[2] Granting that categorizing philosophers into traditions can be a precarious venture, once we have identified philosophers belonging to distinct traditions, and articulated a question or theme that invites their comparison, we are in a position to do comparative philosophy.

We are now brought to the question of why we would want to be in such a position. What is to be gained from comparative philosophy? On one view, the answer to this question is virtually the same as to the question "What is to be gained from philosophy?" If we have a good reason for doing philosophy, it follows that we have a good reason to do comparative philosophy. Whatever our philosophical question, it would seem at least potentially beneficial to compare approaches and responses to the question borne from more than just one tradition. For example, we might seek guidance in answering the question "How should I live?" Confining ourselves to one tradition equips us with less input, yielding a narrower perspective than we might have if we were to expand our purview. Suppose that Tradition A offers a response to this question, or even a set of responses. Suppose that Tradition B offers at least one alternative. Comparing responses from Tradition A with those from Tradition B could prove useful in helping to respond to the mutually engaged question. Of course, there is much to be said for plumbing the depths of a single tradition, and perhaps those with expertise in the philosophies that they are comparing will be capable of the most sophisticated comparative philosophy. The point is that more information is usually helpful, and comparing approaches and positions from different philosophical traditions is one way of obtaining more information.

In addition to having more information to work with when confronting a philosophical problem, comparative philosophy can help us to understand philosophical traditions other than those with which we are most familiar. Suppose that Tradition A is our "home tradition," or that with which we are most familiar. Becoming acquainted with Tradition B via the pursuit of a question asked by both traditions can be enriching not just with respect to our thought about that question but also with respect to one's knowledge of the alternative tradition. The shared question "How should I live?" can serve as an entrée from Tradition A to Tradition B (or vice versa). Starting from this common ground, we can begin to fill out our knowledge of the other tradition. This process might include increasing the nodes of comparison between the compared traditions. As we do so, our judgment of the degree of distance between the traditions may undergo vicissitudes. Just as we cultivate a keener sense of the differences between traditions, we also come to appreciate similarities between traditions. Sometimes we find that traditions we thought to be very alike are, upon further inspection, more different than anticipated. Conversely, sometimes we find that traditions we thought to be very different are in at least some way(s), surprisingly similar.

Comparative philosophy also has the potential to reveal unnoticed or underappreciated aspects of the more familiar tradition. Suppose again that Tradition A is our home tradition. Just as we learn more about Tradition B when we engage with it comparatively, this comparative engagement could lead to new knowledge about Tradition A. Perhaps there is a feature of Tradition B's approach to the question "How should I live?" that is particularly significant to adherents of Tradition B. It is a feature that does not figure prominently in our approach, as adherents to Tradition A. Still, when comparing the two traditions, we come to realize that this feature is to some degree implicit in our approach. Thus, we have acquired insight about our own tradition that might not have been possible without the stimulus of comparison.

Comparative philosophy often leads to creative responses to philosophical problems. Insights from one tradition might be blended or paired with insights from another to provide an innovative approach or response to a philosophical problem. Perhaps the approaches and responses to "How should I live?" coming from Tradition A have been compelling, but they have seemed to leave something out. Perhaps, too, the approaches and responses to this question coming from Tradition B seem to us intriguing but insufficient. Assuming that to do so does not lead to incorrigible contradiction, we may blend or unite the insights of Tradition A and Tradition B, creating an approach or response to the question the likes of which would have been impossible had we confined ourselves to Tradition A.

Scholars have employed a variety of methodologies of comparative philosophy. Canvassing these methods exhaustively would carry me beyond the scope of this study.[3] I think that there is much to admire, however, in the notions of "rooted global philosophy" and "constructive engagement" put forward by Stephen C. Angle. By "rooted global philosophy," Angle means "to work within a particular live philosophical tradition—thus its rootedness—but to do so in a way that is open to stimulus and insights from other philosophical traditions—thus its global nature."[4] By "constructive engagement," Angle means the work to "understand other traditions in their own terms, and find grounds on which we can engage one another constructively."[5] In this book, I work within two live philosophical traditions, Confucianism and American philosophy. I do my best to understand each tradition in its own terms and find grounds on which they can engage one another constructively. Indeed, each chapter of this book represents a separate ground of constructive engagement between Confucianism and American philosophy.

It is my belief that each of the benefits of comparative philosophy that I have discussed may be reaped from the dialogue of Confucianism and American philosophy. Considering the two philosophical traditions in tandem provides us with more robust philosophical resources than if we confined ourselves to only one, considering these traditions together enables us to learn more about each tradition, and considering these traditions together can yield novel approaches to challenging questions, intermingling insights from each.

AMERICAN PHILOSOPHY AS WORLD PHILOSOPHY

In "Reflections on American Philosophy," a chapter of his *The Highroad Around Modernism*, Robert Cummings Neville raises a compelling question: "By name, American philosophy is a national or ethnic philosophy. Is it more than that? Is it a world philosophy that can have power and relevance beyond its place and period of origin?"[6] Although "world philosophy" is, on Neville's own account, "an approximation at best," a philosophy may be described as such if it "can engage and has something to contribute to the work of any major philosophic endeavor in the world, East or West, North or South, elite or unprivileged."[7] With this notion of "world philosophy" in mind, Neville suggests that his question may be answered in the affirmative. On his view, the existential situations that have given rise to the tradition of American philosophy obtain or have analogues in the existential situations that have given rise to other traditions. Consequently, there is potential for American philosophy to participate in fruitful cross-cultural dialogue with other philosophical traditions.

There is, of course, considerable irony in asking whether American philosophy can be a world philosophy. "From the early philosophers of the American constitution through Emerson to Dewey and Whitehead," Neville notes, "American philosophy has been taken to be a creative innovation resulting from the absorption and transformation of many traditions originating outside of America."[8] If American culture is to be viewed as a "melting pot" of people from a variety of ethnic, racial, and religious backgrounds, so ought American philosophy. The traditions that have been absorbed and transformed by American philosophy include virtually all of those that might be lumped under the heading of European philosophy. It has never been controversial to claim that American philosophers were influenced by their contact with Ancient Greek philosophy, European philosophies of the medieval and Enlightenment periods, or the German idealism of the nineteenth century.

In contrast, it has not always been acknowledged that Asian traditions have played a role in the shaping of American philosophy. When the influence has been recognized, it has often been marginalized. In recent years, increasing interest in cross-cultural philosophical dialogue has coincided with amplified recognition of Asian influences upon American philosophy. Moreover, where direct streams of influence are unable to be established, scholars have identified conceptual consonances between Asian philosophies and American philosophy. Much of the discussion has centered on points of contact between philosophies of India and America.[9] As the title of one recent book suggests (Philip Goldberg's *American Veda: From Emerson and the Beatles to Yoga and Meditation—How Indian Spirituality Changed the West*),[10] the reach of Indian philosophies into the American collective consciousness has been broad indeed. While Goldberg's book showcases points of contact between Hinduism and American philosophy, several others have brought to view the historical and theoretical intersections of Buddhism with American philosophy.[11] In comparison, far fewer treatments have been given to comparable connections between American philosophy and philosophies originating in China (i.e., Daoism and Confucianism). Of these, Daoism has received more attention, perhaps owing to affinities shared with Buddhism. The proliferation of popular book titles starting with *Zen and the Art of . . .* and *The Dao (Tao) of . . .* attest to increasing curiosity and awareness of these traditions among Western audiences. Confucianism has not enjoyed comparable attention. I concur with Angle in suspecting that this lack of similar attention to Confucianism derives from its being "seen as more narrowly linked to Chinese culture."[12] Like Angle, I regard this perspective as an unfortunate misperception. This book challenges the notion that Confucianism is exclusively linked to Chinese culture (or East Asian cultures, for that matter), by tracing a broad but interrelated set of historical and conceptual links with American thought.

When referring to Confucian philosophy, I intend the philosophy of Confucius (551–479 BC) and the philosophers most prominently recognized as following in his philosophical footsteps, Mencius

(372–289 BC) and Xunzi (314–217 BC). When referring to American philosophy, I intend the philosophy of those associated with the American Transcendentalist and Pragmatist movements, generally understood as beginning with the philosophical career of Ralph Waldo Emerson (1803–1882) and ending sometime around the time of the death of John Dewey (1859–1952). American Transcendentalism and Pragmatism are sometimes referred to together as Classical American philosophy. For the sake of concision, and consistent with common practice in scholarship, I will simply use "American philosophy" and "American philosophers" when referring to the arc of these intellectual movements and the figures comprising them. In this book, I focus on American philosophers who were based in New England: Ralph Waldo Emerson (1803–1882), Henry David Thoreau (1817–1862), Charles Peirce (1839–1914), William James (1842–1910), and Josiah Royce (1855–1916). One reason for this emphasis is that most of the existing scholarship engaging with Confucianism and American philosophy has taken up American philosophers based in Chicago. While this group includes figures such as George Herbert Mead (1863–1931) and Jane Addams (1860–1935),[13] the philosopher most discussed in this scholarship is undoubtedly Dewey. This scholarship is an important precedent to my own, and it merits a brief review.

CONFUCIUS AND DEWEY

Without question, the philosophies of Confucius and Dewey have occupied the lion's share of comparative work between Confucian and American philosophical traditions. There are good reasons for this. Dewey is unique among Classical American philosophers,[14] insofar as he alone spent time in China (1919–1921).[15] While on a sabbatical leave in Japan, Dewey was invited to China by Hu Shih. Hu had been Dewey's student at Columbia University, thanks to a scholarship drawn from indemnity funds following the Boxer Uprising. As the nexus between Dewey and China, Hu is a pivotal figure.[16] Enjoying immense popularity among the Chinese, Dewey was dubbed a "Second Confucius." In his *John Dewey, Confucius, and Global Philosophy*,

Joseph Grange explains that a major reason for Dewey's being a "Second Confucius" is that he, like Confucius,

> saw experience as the forge within which personal and social change could be welded anew. Change is not easy. Transition to better states of being is a unique cultural event. Traditions wisely understood and creatively used are the background against which reconstruction can be successfully undertaken. Confucius was the sage who saw the necessity of carrying this out on a wide social scale. Dewey envisaged a similar reform effort more than twenty-five hundred years later.[17]

In Hu one finds historical precedent for contemporary scholarly efforts to bridge what might appear *prima facie* an insurmountable gap between Dewey's notions of democracy with traditional Chinese (e.g., Confucian) sociopolitical frameworks. In Grange one finds such a contemporary effort, with the outlining of several "working connections" between Confucius's and Dewey's philosophies.

Two of the most significant contemporary engagements of the social-political philosophies of Confucius and Dewey are David L. Hall and Roger T. Ames's *The Democracy of the Dead: Dewey, Confucius, and the Hope for Democracy in China* and Sor-hoon Tan's *Confucian Democracy: A Deweyan Reconstruction*. The fact that Dewey's notion of democracy was changed by his visit to China is useful to these projects, which import Deweyan notions of democracy into contemporary Chinese life, contending that such a move is not as radical as it might initially seem. Indeed, Hall and Ames insist, following Dewey, that democracy is not about institutions and governments; it is about communities. They suggest, "The principal obstacle to the realization of *effective* democracy in both Asia and the West lies in the failure to recognize this central fact."[18] Moreover, they find that there is "much in the relational definition of human being found in the Confucian tradition that may be favorably compared to the major tenets of Dewey's understanding of the democratic individual."[19] Because both Confucianism and Deweyan Pragmatism promote a rethinking of the dominant Western notion of autonomous individuality, they can be a compelling conceptual inspiration for a democratic vision in China.

Tan further develops the arguments of Hall and Ames, stressing that Confucian and Deweyan philosophies are not only coincident, they are worthy ethico-political ideals. According to Tan, Dewey's understanding "of what government by the people means, what democratic participation requires, and how cooperative inquiry should proceed facilitates the reconstruction of Confucianism in support of democracy."[20] Meanwhile, this comparative engagement sheds new light on Dewey's philosophy:

> Though he insists on flexibility of political forms and the necessity to pay as much attention to the content that affects the functioning of political forms, Dewey has been rather vague about the cultural processes that give content to political forms. In this regard, Confucianism, which traditionally has been more concerned with cultural processes than with political forms, offers new possibilities for accomplishing Dewey's task.[21]

Thus, Confucianism and Dewey's Pragmatism constitute a mutually elucidating and fortifying conceptual tandem.[22]

Notwithstanding the merits of the meeting and merging of the thought of Confucius and Dewey, the predominance of this pairing, at the exclusion of other possible comparative engagements, has prompted uneasiness on the part of some scholars. In the preface to a special issue dedicated to American Pragmatism and Chinese philosophy, the editor-in-chief of the *Journal of Chinese Philosophy*, Chung-ying Cheng, expresses disappointment at the failure of the invited authors to get beyond the comparison to Dewey. He decries that the authors "went the easy way and focused on Dewey as *the* representative of American philosophy."[23] The same kind of lament can be made regarding references to Confucianism that reduce this broad category to the philosophy attributed to Confucius, ignoring developments promulgated by multiple generations of successive Confucians. In the cases of both Confucianism and American philosophy, no one thinker exhaustively represents the tradition. Within each tradition there exists a vast variety of ideas, including instances of internal conflict. When Confucianism is reduced to Confucius, and American philosophy is reduced to Dewey, a wealth of potential for comparative engagement between Confucianism and American philosophy is left untapped.

BROADENING A COMPARATIVE HORIZON

Scholars who *have* engaged with the traditions of Confucianism and American philosophy more broadly have usually argued that they are mutually elucidating and mutually reinforcing.[24] While the predominant focus has been on Confucianism and American Pragmatism, there is little reason to think that the aspects of American Pragmatism that have appealed to these scholars are not also to be found in American Transcendentalism. Richard Shusterman has suggested that "perhaps the most central and comprehensive" of themes shared by Chinese philosophy (including Confucianism) and American Pragmatism is humanism, "the insistence that philosophy is inevitably shaped by the human condition and human purposes and that it should be primarily directed to the aims of preserving, cultivating, and perfecting human life."[25] In this vein, Daniel J. Stephens has offered a constructive engagement of Confucianism and American Pragmatism focused on "practicality, the experiential basis and focus of knowledge and philosophy, and the idea of philosophy as an individually transforming human practice."[26] Similarly, Haiming Wen has stated, "Confucian pragmatism is the philosophical point of view that human beings are able to create valuable relationships through a better understanding of the nature of co-creativity."[27] Concurring with the findings of each of these scholars, in this book, I hope to elucidate lines of influence from Confucianism to American philosophy and to reveal deep conceptual affinities across these apparently disparate philosophical traditions. If this venture should prove successful, it will have effected the broadening of a comparative horizon shared by Confucianism and American philosophy.[28] As evidenced by the scholarly work that I have drawn upon to this point, I am preceded by a number of people in thinking that this horizon can and should be broadened. One set of scholars warrants separate discussion, those working under the banner of Boston Confucianism.

BOSTON CONFUCIANISM

Boston Confucianism refers to a current intellectual movement committed to transporting and adapting Confucianism to locales beyond Asia. The central idea is that Confucianism can be adopted and practiced outside of its geographical roots in much the same way that other major philosophical and religious traditions (e.g., Platonism, Christianity, Buddhism) have proven to be. In other words, Confucianism is a world philosophy.[29] Although there are "New Confucians" based in various other geographical areas, a group of three scholars spearheaded Boston Confucianism: Tu Weiming of Harvard University, and John Berthrong and Robert C. Neville of Boston University. Judging by the account of Berthrong, Boston Confucianism is not *essentially* tied to Boston Pragmatism, but it arose because "Confucianism has become a topic of serious intellectual enquiry in the contemporary cultural scene in Boston."[30] So, what is *essentially* Bostonian about Boston Confucianism is that a collection of individuals identifying as Confucians are based in Boston. Were the Boston Confucians to migrate to another city, the movement would presumably take on a different moniker.[31] Indeed, "Confucianism will take on a distinctive modality in Boston or Toronto . . . or London or Paris."[32]

For his own part, Neville avers, "Boston Confucianism properly focuses on the moral implications of the pragmatic theory of signs in its emphasis on ritual propriety" and that "[j]ust as Neo-Confucianism in the Song and Ming dynasties learned from the Buddhists and Daoists, Boston Confucianism learns from the pragmatists."[33] By drawing upon Peirce's semiotics, Neville identifies an American Pragmatist strand of Boston Confucianism.[34] At the same time, he stipulates, "One must take this discussion of Boston Confucianism with a large sense of humor. The fact that Charles Peirce and Tu Weiming are Bostonians is sheerly accidental, and I mean to be speaking for a wide range of people in American and Asia who approach Confucianism as a portable world philosophy."[35] Consonant with Berthrong's account, Neville explains that Boston Confucianism "includes anyone who treats Confucianism as an important resource for philosophical problems of cultures outside the East Asian sphere, particularly modern Western urban cultures (such as Boston's)."[36]

Boston Confucianism has not exclusively sought to integrate the philosophical traditions of Confucianism and American Pragmatism. As demonstrated in the closing chapter of Neville's book about Boston Confucianism ("Confucianism, Christianity, and Multiple Religious Identity"),[37] Boston Confucianism seems to place more emphasis upon the fruits that may be reaped from the interaction between Confucianism and Christianity than that between Confucianism and American Pragmatism. Consequently, despite the provocative ideas put forth under the heading of Boston Confucianism, many potentially fruitful points of convergence between Confucianism and Classical Boston Pragmatism are overlooked. This is to say nothing of affinities between Confucianism and American Transcendentalism, an intellectual movement that had its roots in the Boston area.[38] Of course, it is the central aim of the present work to rectify the relative paucity of attention that has been paid to both American Transcendentalism and classical Boston Pragmatism in comparative studies of Confucianism and American philosophy.

TEXTUAL CONVENTIONS

When it comes to the Confucian texts engaged in this study, I have had to select from a vast number of available translations. My decisions concerning translations have been guided by two considerations—accuracy and literary quality. Clearly, it is important that a translation be accurate. Literary quality is also important, for a translation succeeds to the extent that it conveys the meaning of the original text in the language of the intended audience. Of course, there is a wide expanse of time and culture between Warring States China (475–221

BC), during which Mencius and Xunzi lived (and during which it is believed the *Analects* was first written) and twenty-first-century America. Translators of Confucian texts (and classical Chinese texts generally) are agreed that several significant concepts in these texts lack a neat correlate in English. Effective translations navigate this delicate situation carefully, finding a way to convey accurately (or as accurately as possible) what is meant in the original text, despite what may be dramatic differences between the milieu in which the text originated and the milieu in which the reader is situated. In this work, I primarily follow the translation of the *Analects* by Edward Slingerland (2003), the translation of the *Mencius* by Irene Bloom (2009), and the translation of the *Xunzi* (2003) by Burton Watson. On the whole, I find these translations satisfy the aforementioned criteria. I do, however, occasionally draw upon alternate translations. Indeed, when discussing translations of Confucian texts that were read by classical American thinkers, I must! On all such occasions, I make a note of the translation that I am consulting, and when it is not obvious, I indicate my rationale for doing so.

I make minor modifications to some passages in the aforementioned translations, following the convention of Roger T. Ames and Henry Rosemont, Jr., in leaving some key concepts from the Chinese untranslated.[39] In these cases, I resist settling on an English term that would, in my view, inadequately express the meaning(s) of the term. Consider *ren* (仁). This *ren* is distinct from *ren* (人), or "person," although the latter graph combines with the graph for *er* (二), or "two," to make the graph for *ren* (仁). Ames and Rosemont hold that this etymological analysis "underscores the Confucian assumption that one cannot become a person by oneself—we are, from our inchoate beginnings, irreducibly social."[40] Among translations of *ren* (仁) one finds: humaneness, humanity, benevolence, authoritative conduct, goodness, and Slingerland's translation, Goodness (he also capitalizes the *r* in *Ren*, further distinguishing the term from *ren* 人). This cluster of concepts is basically coherent; one can at least infer that *ren* is a positive moral quality, and perhaps a fundamental one. Nonetheless, it is difficult to state precisely what *ren* is. Perhaps *ren* is all of these things (and perhaps more), contingent on context. Perhaps, too, *ren* was undergoing transformation during the time of (or even in the hands of) Confucius, Mencius, or Xunzi. Rather than select a single English word, with connotations that the contemporary reader might struggle to keep separate from the classical Chinese context, I choose to allow *ren* to remain *ren*.[41]

OVERVIEW

In the first two chapters of this book, I focus on Confucianism and American Transcendentalism. The first chapter takes up the thought of Emerson; the second chapter takes up the thought of Thoreau. Emerson and Thoreau are distinct from Peirce, James, and Royce not simply because they are Transcendentalists while the others are Pragmatists. Importantly, in the cases of both Emerson and Thoreau, there is clear evidence of their having directly engaged with early translations of Confucian texts. Quotes from or allusions to Confucian texts in their published works, reading journals, and private correspondence all stand as clear testaments to their awareness of and interest in ideas from the Confucian tradition. Egbert S. Oliver is correct when stating,

> Emerson came at a momentous time in world history, when the East and the West were awakening to a realization that each needed the other, when the old nations of the Orient were opening their doors to commerce in materials of usefulness and beauty and to the intercommunication of intellect and spirit. Emerson was one of the first Americans to venture into the literature of Asia and absorb it sufficiently to be an early interpreter.[42]

I would amend Oliver's quote in just one way—inserting after each instance of "Emerson" the words "and Thoreau."

In chapter 1, I examine the philosophies of friendship found in the thought of Confucius and Emerson. This focus is suggested by Emerson's recurrent quoting, in journals and in published works, a sentence of Confucius's: "Have no friend unlike yourself." I ask what precisely Confucius means by this, and what Emerson's appropriation of Confucius's remark means to him. I show that Emerson's relationship to Confucius on this point is marked by an interesting ambivalence; earlier in his interactions with Confucius's thought, he distances himself from the view, while later, he seems to position himself much more closely to it.

A similar ambivalence animates Thoreau's disposition toward Confucian thought, as I demonstrate in chapter 2. It can be argued that Thoreau was even more eager a reader of available translations of Confucian texts than Emerson, for there is clear evidence of Thoreau's having read not only the English translations of Confucian classics that were available to him but also having read and partially translated, in one of his private journals, a French translation into English.[43] I engage with Thoreau's notebook as I consider the extent to which Thoreau's "Civil Disobedience" may have been shaped by his contact with the thought of Confucius and Mencius. I show that although Thoreau explicitly opposes ideas he associates with Confucian thought, he is more Confucian in "Civil Disobedience" than he lets on, or than he realizes. Included in this analysis is indication of passages of "Civil Disobedience" in which it seems fairly clear that Thoreau is invoking ideas from Confucius and Mencius that were recorded in his notebook, despite his not making explicit that he is doing so.

The following three chapters are comparative engagements of Confucianism with American Pragmatism, particularly the thought of Peirce, James, and Royce. Unlike the cases of Emerson and Thoreau, there is little in the way of evidence of Peirce, James, or Royce having direct contact with the classic Confucian texts. Nonetheless, conceptual affinities between the thought of Confucian philosophers and the thought of these American philosophers can certainly be identified. Whereas part of my approach in the first two chapters is to investigate lines of influence, my methodology in these chapters is more centered on locating conceptual affinities and deploying them to either contribute productively to ongoing debates about an aspect of a philosopher's thought or to elucidate an unclear aspect of one thinker through the prism of the other. Scholars of comparative philosophy working in the West often seek to "translate" the East through the concepts and theories of Western philosophy, motivated by the desire to demystify and legitimize Asian philosophies in the eyes of Western scholars who are unfamiliar with, or skeptical of the value of, Asian philosophies. I am not immune from the practice of "translating" Confucian philosophy in the language of American philosophy, but I also attempt in my comparative engagements to "translate" American philosophy in Confucian terms. When it is most effective, comparative philosophy is *mutually* elucidating for each participant in the comparison.

Employing the conceptual framework of Peirce's famous essay "The Fixation of Belief," in chapter 3, I examine the character of Confucius's habits of inquiry and belief formation. This approach is inspired by the current debate concerning whether Confucius (and by extension, Confucianism) is better understood as authoritarian or authoritative. Examination of Confucius's normative views concerning inquiry and belief reveals significant insight into how he is oriented toward diversity of opinion and deliberation in a communal context. As I proceed, I weigh in on debate within scholarship of each figure concerning how best to understand pertinent aspects of their thought, with strides made in comprehension of Peirce's thought, as well. The hermeneutical potential in a rapprochement of Peirce with Confucius may be especially intriguing to the rapidly growing network of Peirce scholars in China, where "The Fixation of Belief" (among other papers by Peirce) has been translated and closely studied.[44]

In chapter 4, I offer a comparative analysis of Mencius and Xunzi, on one hand, and James, on the other. All three of these philosophers were acutely interested in human psychology and morality. Although "moral psychology" is a term that has come into vogue well after the times of these thinkers, it is certainly a principal philosophical preoccupation of each. Well known is the apparently diametrical opposition represented by the views of Mencius and Xunzi, with the former usually being described as thinking human nature to be fundamentally good, and the latter usually being described as thinking human nature to be fundamentally bad. While this depiction of their views ignores important nuances, the vocabularies that they provide to discuss the morality of human nature and the project of moral cultivation are quite useful when considering James's philosophy. For all that James wrote of human nature, his take on the morality of human nature and the nature of moral development is difficult to pinpoint. I maintain that it is possible to better understand the thought of James when guided by the thought of Mencius and Xunzi. Likewise, a comparative engagement with the thought of James brings into sharper focus the important areas of continuity and discontinuity between Mencius and Xunzi.

Having just discussed human nature and moral development, in chapter 5, I address human behavior in the aftermath of wrongdoing. In particular, I focus on the situation of the wrongdoer, the phenomenon of shame experienced by the wrongdoer, and the obligations incumbent on the wrongdoer in the wake of his wrongdoing. Here I place into dialogue the thought of Confucius, Mencius, and Royce.[45] These thinkers have in common a keen attunement to the types of shame people experience, and they hold similar views concerning which features of one's conduct and character justify or call for feelings of shame. Moreover, each of these thinkers finds paramount the need to acknowledge one's wrongdoing and redouble one's efforts at moral cultivation. This includes making amends for one's wrongdoing. I canvass a number of theories of atonement and identify two theories of atonement that seem to be at work in, and held in common by, Confucian thought and Royce's philosophy.

I conclude with reflections on directions that might be taken in the future to build upon the foundations of previously published scholarship and the present work. Confucianism and American philosophy are traditions teeming in wisdom and insights of both historical interest and contemporary value. I hope that this study will make a meaningful contribution to the worlds of Confucian philosophy and American philosophy and deepen the nexus between the two. I hope, too, that other scholars will join me in broadening this comparative horizon.

1

Confucianism and Emerson

Friendship

INTRODUCTION

Emerson's awareness of Confucianism appears as early as a journal entry of 1824, "Indeed, the light of Confucius goes out in translation into the language of Shakespear[e] & Bacon."[1] Records show that Emerson borrowed Joshua Marshman's *The Works of Confucius: Containing the Original Text with a Translation*[2] from the Boston Athenaeum February 16 to March 1, 1836.[3] Excerpts from Emerson's *Journals* dated March 3, 1836, feature dozens of "Sentences of Confucius."[4] In 1843, upon further contact with Confucius via David Collie's complete translation of *The Four Books*,[5] Emerson again quoted Confucius in his journals.[6] That same year, Emerson and Thoreau collected and published quotes from Confucius in two installments of their coedited "Ethnical Scriptures" column of *The Dial*.[7] In 1863, Emerson continued his study of the Confucian classics, reading James Legge's translation of the *Confucian Analects, the Great Learning, and the Doctrine of the Mean*,[8] again excerpting sayings from Confucius in his journals.[9] In a speech at the banquet in honor of the Chinese embassy in Boston in 1868, Emerson summarizes the significance of Confucius in laudatory comparison:

Confucius has not yet gathered all his fame. When Socrates heard that the oracle declared that he was the wisest of men, he said, it must mean that other men held that they were wise, but that he knew that he knew nothing. Confucius had already affirmed this of himself: and what we call the GOLDEN RULE of Jesus, Confucius had uttered in the same terms five hundred years before. His morals, though addressed to a state of society unlike ours, we read with profit to-day.[10]

Despite such clear evidence of Emerson's interest in Confucian philosophy, only passing attention has been paid to the Confucian influence upon Emerson's thought. When the subject has been treated, most scholars have downplayed or even denied a philosophical influence, maintaining that Emerson's interest in Confucianism was only superficial.[11]

A broad range of scholars has perpetuated the view that Confucianism was of marginal influence upon Emerson's thought. John Jay Chapman writes in *Emerson, and Other Essays* (1899), "The East added nothing to Emerson, but gave him a few trappings of speech."[12] John S. Harrison corroborates this view in *The Teachers of Emerson* (1910), forecasting, "When the influence of Emerson's Oriental readings come to be worked out in all its details, it may be shown that they colored the manner of his speech."[13] In *Emerson and Asia* (1931), Frederic Ives Carpenter asserts that with respect to Chinese philosophers, Emerson "never actually incorporated their thought into his own writing, but merely quoted the sayings of Confucius, Mencius, and the rest, externally, as illustrations of his ideas."[14] In *The Oriental Religions and American Thought* (1981), Carl T. Jackson states, "whenever [Emerson] spoke of Asia, he usually meant India,"[15] conceding that Emerson "admired Confucius, but did not feel the same toward Chinese religion generally."[16] More recently, Richard Grossman claims in *The Tao of Emerson* (2007), "Emerson and Confucius were linked by their common belief in what Emerson called 'the infinitude of the Asiatic soul,'"[17] while stipulating, "But in practice, Confucianism was not a philosophy to which Emerson could have wholly subscribed, since it was almost exclusively concerned with societal structure, worldly transactions, codified rules of behavior, and what might be called patriarchal politics."[18]

Of course, influence does not require wholesale subscription. Wide reaches of Emerson's thought could very well be compatible with, or influenced by, his contact with Confucianism, even if the totality of his thought is not. Commenting in 1942 on likenesses in style of composition and thought, Lin Yutang asserts, "Generally, the reader will find reading Chinese philosophers like reading Emerson."[19] Arthur Christy identifies a deeper affinity, claiming in *The Orient in American Transcendentalism* (1932), "The Confucian, or Chinese, parallel is to be found in Emerson's ethical writings."[20] In a doctoral dissertation provocatively titled "Emerson, the American Confucius: An Exploration of Confucian Motifs in the Early Writings (1830–1843) of Ralph Waldo Emerson" (2013), Kyle Bryant Simmons claims, "Confucian motifs can stand side-by-side with all other thinkers that Emerson read, not dismissed or divided from them, like most investigations have attempted."[21] It is the views of these scholars with which I am aligned. The discussion of friendship in this chapter may serve as an illustration of the Confucian parallel in Emerson's early ethical writings.

My point of departure is one short but compelling quote from Marshman's translation of the *Analects* that Emerson continually returned to: "Have no friend unlike yourself."[22] This remark, appearing in *Analects* 1.8 and 9.25, made more than a passing impression on Emerson.[23] In addition to its appearance in his journals (1836) and prior to its inclusion in *The Dial* (1843), he had used it in his "Society" lecture, delivered at the Masonic Temple in Boston, January 26, 1837. For much of that lecture, Emerson seems to endorse the dictum "Have no friend unlike yourself." Interestingly, however, his quoting of Confucius initiates a pivot from ruminating on the delight of friendship with one who is like oneself, to admitting the elusiveness of such relationships, and making the concession that their rareness necessitates broadening the scope of those whom we befriend. Confucius's words thus simultaneously capture something Emerson thinks to be true about friendship and signal something he wants to move beyond.

In this chapter, I will attempt to gain a clearer picture of compatibility between Emerson's thought and Confucian thought about friendship. I will first consider Emerson's comments about friendship in "Society." Then, I will examine remarks about friendship found in the *Analects*, some attributed to Confucius, others attributed to followers of Confucius. Finally, I will take up Emerson's "Friendship" essay (1841). I argue that while in "Society" Emerson seems to distance himself from Confucius's thought about friendship, a broader view taking account of the *Analects* as a whole and Emerson's more mature thought on friendship reveals more convergence than divergence between Confucian and Emersonian thought on friendship.

"HAVE NO FRIEND UNLIKE YOURSELF"

"Have no friend unlike yourself" appears first in *Analects* 1.8. Here I reproduce Marshman's translation of the passage—the translation with which Emerson was most familiar during his writing of both the "Society" lecture and the "Friendship" essay: "Chee says, an honorable man, without dignity of conduct, can obtain no respect. His learning cannot remain stable. Set the highest value on faithfulness and sincerity. Have no friend unlike yourself. Transgressing, you should not fear to return."[24] "Chee," a term that Marshman connects with "chief," is rendered "Master" in contemporary translations (i.e., "Chee says" is "The Master said"). It is understood that Confucius is the speaker in passages with this beginning. "Have no friend unlike yourself" is rendered "do not accept as a friend one who is not your equal" by Slingerland, and "Do not have as a friend anyone who is as good as you are" by Ames and Rosemont. In this passage, Confucius connects friendship with learning and virtue, suggesting that having a friend unlike oneself (or, not as good as oneself) will imperil one's learning and the quality of one's character.

In order to appreciate the ambivalent position that this quote from Confucius occupies for Emerson in "Society," we should take stock of the contexts immediately before and after the quote in that essay. Ahead of the quote, Emerson relates to his audience the benefits of keeping company with those with whom one can act naturally:

> A man should live among those people among whom he can act naturally. Among those who permit and provoke the expression of all his thoughts and emotions. Among such only can there be one soul. . . . Then his education goes on and he is becoming greater; and not when he acts a constrained part in company which gratifies his ambition: then, his education stops; then, he is becoming less.[25]

At the same time that Emerson extols the value of living among those with whom one can act naturally and describes the ideal fellowship as the forging of "one soul," he resists the notion that we should have no friends unlike ourselves. Emerson's next words are his quote of Confucius:

> "Have no friend," said Confucius, "unlike yourself." Yet, on the other part, the claims of the ignorant and uncultivated must always find some allowance. The course of events does steadily thwart any attempt at very dainty and select fellowship, and he who would live as a man in the world, must take notice, that the likeminded shall not often be sent him; that the unlikeminded can teach him much; that Apollo sojourns always with the herdmen of Admetus; that he must not be too much a utilitarian, with too exact calculation of profit and loss, but must toss his odors round broadcast to the Divinity, heedless if they fall upon the altar or upon the ground, for all the world is God's altar. Let him not wait too proudly for the presence of the gifted and the good.[26]

Emerson contrasts the ideal of finding fellowship with the gifted and the good with the value to be had in fellowship with the unlikeminded, tempering the position taken to this point. Circumstances may be such that likeminded gifted and/or good individuals are not accessible. Because friendship is a crucial good, it is worthwhile to accept lesser, unlikeminded, individuals as friends. Such friendships serve us better than having none at all. All the world is God's altar; all people can teach us much.

Notice that in each of the passages quoted, Emerson appraises the value to be gained from a friendship in terms of how much one can learn from it. In the company of those with whom we can act naturally, education happens and we are better for it. It is "when he acts a constrained part" with others that the individual's education stops and he becomes less. The ignorant and uncultivated (i.e., the unlike-minded) can teach the individual much, so it is imprudent to wait too proudly for the gifted and good (who presumably would be more adept teachers). But what, precisely, do we learn from our friends? Perhaps surprisingly, we learn from our friends about ourselves:

> Whilst we sat alone, we could not arouse ourselves to thought, but sitting with a friend in the stimulated activity of the faculties, we lay bare to ourselves our own mystery, and start at the total loneliness and infinity of one man. We see that man serves man only to acquaint him with himself, but into that high sanctuary, no person can enter. Lover and friend are as remote from it as enemies.[27]

It seems unusual that what we gain from friendship is the capacity to "lay bare to ourselves our own mystery," to acquaint ourselves with ourselves. It seems that such revelations would occur in solitude, for being in the company of others poses the possibility of distracting us from such revelations. Still, Emerson believes that we harbor unseen potentialities that only our friends will draw out of us. Moreover, while friends who are our intellectual and moral equal are optimal (presuming that we are not among the "ignorant and uncultivated"), those who are lesser than us may still suffice to achieve the aims of friendship.

When it comes to whom we can befriend, how sharp is the difference between Confucius and Emerson? Confucius and Emerson both acknowledge the possibility of friendship with those who are "unlike ourselves," though Confucius apparently does not concede their possible benefit. But is this accurate? Is Emerson right in thinking that he is parting ways from Confucius's view? Later in this chapter, I will add to the account so far given of Emerson's thought about friendship, focusing on the more explicit and sustained discussion found in "Friendship." Next, however, I will turn to Confucius.

CONFUCIAN FRIENDSHIP

In the *Analects*, we are immediately introduced to Confucius's thought about friendship:

> *Analects* 1.1: The Master said, "To learn and then have occasion to practice what you have learned—is this not satisfying? To have friends (*peng* 朋) arrive from afar—is this not a joy? To be patient even when others do not understand—is this not the mark of the *junzi* (君子)?"[28]

This passage invites a host of questions. To start, what do these three sentences have to do with one another? What relationship obtains among (1) learning and having occasion to practice what you have learned, (2) having friends arrive from afar, and (3) being patient even when others do not understand? Next, what sort of people are these friends? What sort of person can properly be said to be a friend? Moreover, what is the nature of the bond shared between friends? What makes a friendship a friendship?

Edward Slingerland cites the Jin dynasty commentator Li Chong (266–316) as holding that "the three activities mentioned in 1.1 refer to the stages of learning: mastering the basics, discussing them with fellow students and working hard at mastering them, and finally becoming a teacher of others."[29] Eric C. Mullis also connects Confucius's comment about friendship with the process of learning, stating that in *Analects* 1.1, "Confucius expresses delight in learning as well as delight when his 'young friends' (*xiaozi* 小子) come from far away to study with him."[30] The former interpretation imagines the friendship as between disciples, whereas the latter imagines the friendship as between master and disciple. Given the likelihood of Confucius's making this remark in the company of his disciples, both of these interpretations are plausible. Each provides a coherent response to the question of how the sentences in the passage are connected to one another. But which is more accurate?

Not all scholars hold that "friends" in this passage should be understood as "young friends," although the idea that Confucius is here referring to friends that are in some sense inferior to oneself is not unique to Mullis. Sor-hoon Tan observes that Confucius's use of "friendship" in *Analects* 1.1 is distinctive: "In the one instance where *peng* occurs alone (*Analects* 1.1), it is in no way deprecated—the joy of a visit from *peng* (even if they are inferior friends) coming from far away is compared to the delight of frequently practicing what one has learnt."[31] This observation is prompted by debate in the scholarship concerning two terms in classical Chinese usually translated as "friend," *peng* (朋) and *you* (友). The first four of the Confucian "Five Relationships"[32] (ruler–subject, father–son, husband–wife, elder brother–younger brother) are unquestionably hierarchical, with the former partner to the relationship being regarded as superior to the latter. The fifth relationship (friend–friend) may also be viewed as hierarchical, if one of *peng* and *you* is regarded as the superior friend and the other as the inferior friend.[33] If the "friend–friend" relationship is understood as analogous to that between brothers, it is not beyond the pale to think that the relationship would be understood as hierarchical. If entirely analogous to the relationship between brothers, the hierarchy would be indexed to age, with the elder friend being superior to the younger. This seems unlikely, however, and I will soon suggest what I think to be relevant consideration for marking out superiority and inferiority within the context of friendship.

If Confucius thinks friendship to be hierarchical, "Have no friend unlike yourself" appears to signal an inconsistency in his thought. But I think it would be hasty to draw such a conclusion. While friends might be superior and inferior *in some sense*, they may be akin to one another *in some other sense*. Tim Connolly observes, "The *Analects* opens by remarking on the joys of friends coming together. Friends also take on a shared commitment to virtue; this can take place even between people of different rank or economic status."[34] This reading is consistent with the view that friendship in *Analects* 1.1 refers to the relationship that Confucius has with his disciples, a relationship that is clearly marked by hierarchy in at least two ways—age (Confucius is older) and wisdom (Confucius is wiser). At the same time, Confucius and his disciples may be said to share a commitment to virtue; it is this shared commitment, presumably, that brings them together in the first place. To receive such a friend (a past disciple, or perhaps a present disciple who has traveled for whatever reason) could indeed be a source of joy, no matter whether the friend is a *peng* as opposed to a *you*.

The question remains as to what exactly Confucius thinks friendship involves. Is Connolly correct that for Confucius, friends take on a shared commitment to virtue? Mullis similarly suggests, "Confucius emphasizes that studying with friends is enjoyable and that one stands to be improved by morally good friends."[35] Tan also states that, for Confucius, "to be a true friend is to bring about, to contribute to, another's ethical development."[36] It is no mere coincidence that each of these three scholars treats Confucius's notion of friendship in tandem with that of Aristotle, whose highest type of friendship, the "perfect friendship," occurs between equally virtuous, morally excellent people. But the foregoing discussion concerning the asymmetrical nature of Confucian friendship suggests an important contrast between Confucian and Aristotelian notions of friendship. Aristotle would claim that the gap in age between master and disciple is joined by a gap in moral development, and that this closes off the possibility of such a friendship being a "perfect friendship." Instead, such a bond would be a friendship of pleasure or a friendship of utility. Although types of friendship nonetheless, they are not the primary type of friendships that we should strive to cultivate. For Confucius, however, the situation is different. Moral development is an essential component of the ideal friendship. If there is a superior party in the friend–friend relationship, then, it is the individual who is more mature morally; the inferior friend is the individual who is less so.

This view is to some extent that of David L. Hall and Roger T. Ames, who explain that in classical Chinese, "Friendship is based upon appreciated differences between oneself and another person that present themselves as specific occasions for one's character development, rather than upon perceived commonalities with the other person."[37] Because the hierarchy within Confucian friendship is indexed to character, Hall and Ames claim, "a Confucian 'friend,' a *you* 友, who is not better than oneself is not properly a friend."[38] Of course, it is plausible to regard Confucius and his disciples as friends, *pengyou* (朋友), who are mutually invested in moral development, and who, through their interactions, help one another develop morally, even if Confucius is the one who formally occupies the role of mentor (*you*), the disciples being the mentees (*peng*).

I want to emphasize *mutual* moral development as a component of Confucius's notion of friendship, rather than *mere* moral development. It is not sufficient that I develop morally as a benefit of my relationship with the other party. Even in hierarchical or asymmetrical friendships, in which I am the inferior party, I can still contribute to the moral development of my friend. By insisting on this point as a crucial element of Confucius's notion of friendship, I differ slightly from Xiufen Lu, whose list of seven "unique aspects of the Confucian concept of friendship" does not include this:

> (a) Friendship is not based on hierarchy—although hierarchies of age and social status are recognized among friends, they do not determine the nature of the relationship between friends—friends may develop mutual respect and bonds in spite of these hierarchies; (b) Friendship is not characterized by sharply defined duties and obligations as are family relations; (c) Friendships, like ideal family relations, however, are characterized by affection, concern, and trust, but they are not structured or shaped by family ties, rather, they are voluntary—friendship, furthermore, has some distinctive characteristics; to wit: (d) Friendship offers a unique type of joy and enjoyment and personal fulfillment; (e) Friendship provides a form of understanding and recognition that cannot be attained in other ways; (f) Friendship involves freely trusting others and being trusted; (g) Friendship is necessary for one's moral cultivation toward the virtue of *ren*. All of these qualities are unique aspects of the Confucian concept of friendship.[39]

I say that I differ slightly from Lu, as Lu comes close to articulating my position with (a) and (g). But I think that (a) must be put more strongly; for Confucius, friends *do* develop mutual respect and bonds in spite of hierarchies. If not, the individuals in question are not truly friends, but simply people interacting with one another. Further, (g) must be clarified. I agree that friendship is necessary for one's moral cultivation toward *ren*. But it should be made clear that it is necessary to be both a giver and a receiver in the context of friendship. Moral cultivation occurs both in what one learns and in what one teaches, and learning and teaching of this kind can happen in virtually any context in which human beings interact.

This portrayal of Confucius's conception of friendship finds support in other passages of the *Analects*. Consider *Analects* 12.24: "Master Zeng said, 'The *junzi* acquires friends (*you*) by means of cultural refinement, and then relies upon his friends (*you*) for support in becoming *ren*.'" Master Zeng was one of Confucius's earliest disciples, and several of the passages in the *Analects* feature him rather than his teacher. Those who compiled the *Analects* must have regarded him as a reliable transmitter of Confucian ideas. Here, Master Zeng succinctly and explicitly expresses the feature of mutuality inherent in moral development between friends. As Slingerland comments, "Friends in virtue are drawn to each other by their common interest in learning and culture—their common love of the *dao* (道)[40]—and then support each other in these endeavors."[41]

That Master Zeng's remark is faithful to Confucius's own thinking can be inferred from *Analects* 15.10:

> Zigong asked about becoming *ren*.
> The Master said, "Any craftsman who wishes to do his job well must first sharpen his tools. In the same way, when living in a given state, one must serve those ministers who are worthy and befriend those scholar-officials who are *ren*."

Confucius's response to his disciple's inquiry about moral cultivation is to stress the necessity of surrounding oneself with worthy and *ren* people. This includes befriending scholar-officials who are *ren*, presumably because of their positive influence. Doing so is analogous to the patient, steady work of a craftsman who sharpens his tools in order to do his job well.

With an echo of "Have no friend unlike yourself," Confucius warns in *Analects* 16.4 that not every friendship is worthwhile:

> Confucius said, "Beneficial types of friendship number three, as do harmful types of friendship. Befriending the upright,

those who are true to their word, or those of broad learning—these are the beneficial types of friendship. Befriending clever flatterers, skillful dissemblers, or the smoothly glib—these are the harmful types of friendship."

This trio—clever flatterers, skillful dissemblers, and the smoothly glib—constitutes a collection of sorts of people who clearly are not conducive to moral development.[42] As Whalen Lai points out, "The reason for avoiding 'lesser' friends is that by their very proximity, they might influence a man's character—for worse."[43] Of course, choosing the right friends is not always easy. It can be difficult to discern the clever flatterer from the sincere giver of praise. Confucius is certainly aware of this problem, intimating the difficulty of selecting appropriate friends in *Analects* 9.30:

> The Master said, "Just because someone is able to learn with you does not necessarily mean that they can travel the *dao* in your company; just because they can travel the *dao* in your company does not necessarily mean that they can take their place alongside you; just because they can take their place alongside you does not necessarily mean that they can join you in employing discretion."

Slingerland suggests that although this passage "is most directly a comment about virtue and friendship . . . its larger purpose is probably to emphasize that the journey of self-cultivation is long and requires many steps."[44] I would argue that these purposes go hand in hand. Self-cultivation is a long and difficult journey, in which friendships figure prominently. Of a piece with other aspects of self-cultivation, navigating one's friendships carefully is crucial. While we do not choose our family, we do choose our friends. These choices are reflective of who we are, and our presence with our chosen company further contributes to the shaping of who we will become.

The *Analects* features several passages highlighting the need to be attuned to the delicate nature of friendship. Consider the following:

Analects 1.4: Master Zeng said, "Every day I examine myself on three counts: in my dealings with others, have I in any way failed to be dutiful? In my interactions with friends and associates, have I in any way failed to be trustworthy? Finally, have I in any way failed to repeatedly put into practice what I teach?

Analects 4.26: Ziyou said, "Being overbearing in service to a lord will lead to disgrace, while in relating to friends and companions it will lead to estrangement."

Analects 12.23: Zigong asked about friendship.
The Master replied, "Reprove your friend when dutifulness requires, but do so gently. If your words are not accepted then desist, lest you incur insult."

In each of these passages, the speaker (Master Zeng, Ziyou, Confucius) treats the subject of scrutiny in the context of friendship. Master Zeng introspects daily on whether he has been trustworthy to his friends. He is a habitual scrutinizer of his own behavior in the context of interpersonal relationships, friendships among them.[45] Ziyou warns that being overbearing to friends will lead to estrangement, implying that scrutinizing the behavior of one's friends can become problematic if taken too far. Confucius essentially says this, too, though his remark explicitly acknowledges the occasional necessity of scrutinizing one's friends. What is critical is balancing this necessity with that of the "support" required in helping a friend to become *ren*.[46]

Recall the questions provoked by *Analects* 1.1. I wondered about the relationship shared among (1) learning and having occasion to practice what you have learned, (2) having friends arrive from afar, and (3) being patient even when others do not understand. Drawing further on the *Analects* and on scholarly commentaries, the close relationship obtaining among these becomes clearer. It is plausible that Confucius refers to his relationship with his disciples in each clause. If so, we have indication that for Confucius, individuals of different positions within a hierarchy—the very hierarchy that gives rise to their interaction—can be friends. Moreover, while education is prominent in the context of Confucius's friendships with disciples, mutual moral development between friends in any context involves learning from one another. There is an affinity, then, between this aspect of Confucian thought about friendship and that of Emerson in "Society."

I also wondered what sort of people friends are, and what sort of bond friendship is. Textual evidence shows that friends are people with whom we are joined on our journey along the *dao*, our journey of moral development or self-cultivation. Again, there is a similarity between this part of Confucian thought about friendship and Emerson's thought in "Society," as Emerson there cites expansion of one's self-knowledge as a main benefit of friendship. Navigating friendships is a delicate and difficult enterprise, requiring careful attunement to oneself and others. While (1) and (3) need not be confined to the context of friendship, it is evident that they are applicable in that arena. At the same time, friendship is a source of joy, and our lives are far better off with friends than without. Although virtually everyone would say this about friendship, this is nonetheless another aspect of compatibility between Confucian thought about friendship and Emerson's thought about friendship in "Society."

CONFUCIANISM IN EMERSON'S "FRIENDSHIP"

I turn now to Emerson's "Friendship" essay, published in *Essays: First Series* (1841). It is here that Emerson gives sustained treatment to the subject of friendship. The tone of "Friendship" vacillates, often coming to rest in a mood dourer than that which one might expect. To be sure, Emerson prizes friendship, but he is also attuned to a range of letdowns that are borne from it. Given its fluctuating mood on the subject, it is difficult to disagree with Russell B. Goodman's summation of "Friendship" as "a meditation or set of variations on [the] theme of hope and disappointment in our lives with others."[47] I will take account of several strands of "Friendship" with the question of compatibility with

Confucius's thought on friendship in mind. In "Society," Emerson's stance toward Confucius's thought on friendship is decidedly ambivalent. Having considered several passages in the *Analects* relevant to friendship, a close reading of Emerson's "Friendship" should furnish a more informed view of how closely the thought of each is related.

The style of "Friendship" is undoubtedly unconventional. George Sebouhian describes Emerson's style as being "intended to force the reader, along with the writer, to engage in dialogue, to slow down, to exclaim, to enter into the irresolution, and not sit in passive expectation of prepared truth."[48] Christopher J. Newfield elaborates on this irresolution, asserting that Emerson "almost never sustains a description of relations between equal men without these relations becoming those of domination or submission."[49] While I think that Newfield overstates the point, it is true that Emerson continually points to incommensurability, be it between friends or between one's idea of one's friend and the friend as he really is.

Also unconventional is Emerson's way of beginning the essay, not by discussing friends, but by musing on the kindness of "the whole human family," marveling at the "many persons we meet in houses, whom we scarcely speak to" and the "many we see in the street, or sit with in church."[50] In the next paragraph, he describes in abstract terms "emotions of benevolence and complacency which are felt toward others,"[51] not pausing to take up a specific example of these emotions felt toward a friend. Continuing in this vein, in the third paragraph, he remarks on anticipating the arrival in one's house of a "commended stranger."[52] Ahead of this visitor's arrival, the "house is dusted, all things fly into their places, the old coat is exchanged for the new."[53] Upon his arrival, we "talk better than we are wont" and engage in "a series of sincere, graceful, rich communications."[54] It is not long, however, before things take a dispiriting turn:

> But as soon as the stranger begins to intrude his partialities, his definitions, his defects, into the conversation, it is all over. He has heard the first, the last and best he will ever hear from us. He is no stranger now. Vulgarity, ignorance, misapprehension

are old acquaintances. Now, when he comes, he may get the order, the dress, and the dinner,—but the throbbing of the heart, and the communications of the soul, no more.[55]

This vignette about how we stand in relation to the stranger introduces a framework through which Emerson will discuss how we stand in relation to our friends. While we might expect for the case of friendship to be set in sharp contrast against the example of the stranger, Emerson draws out more similarity than difference.

Shifting immediately to a more optimistic note in the fourth paragraph, Emerson effusively marvels at the pleasure of "the jets of affection that make a young world for me again" in the "just and firm encounter of two, in a thought, in a feeling."[56] In words that seem to echo and amplify Confucius's comment about the joy of receiving a friend from afar in *Analects* 1.1, Emerson writes, "Let the soul be assured that somewhere in the universe it should rejoin its friend, and it would be content and cheerful alone for a thousand years."[57] In the fifth paragraph, the expressions of appreciation for friendship turn personal. For the first time, Emerson speaks in the first-person singular: "I awoke this morning with devout thanksgiving for my friends, the old and the new. Shall I not call God the Beautiful, who daily showeth himself so to me in his gifts?"[58]

As the essay moves forward, so too do the vicissitudes of Emerson's appraisals of interpersonal relationships. In the sixth paragraph, Emerson confesses, "I have often had fine fancies about persons which have given me delicious hours; but the joy ends in the day: it yields no fruit."[59] In the seventh paragraph, he laments, "Friendship, like the immortality of the soul, is too good to be believed."[60] At the same time, Emerson admits, "every man passes his life in the search after friendship," even if the new friend is best understood as "a delicious torment."[61]

The ebb and flow of Emerson's thought about friendship in this essay is perhaps emblematic of the ebb and flow of his thought on friendship over time. On the subject of whether friendship may occur between individuals unlike one another, Emerson's thinking seems to have evolved since "Society." Now, all friendships involve some degree of likeness and some degree of unlikeness:

> Friendship requires that rare mean betwixt likeness and unlikeness, that piques each with the presence of power and of consent in the other party. Let me be alone to the end of the world, rather than that my friend should overstep, by a word or a look, his real sympathy. I am equally balked by antagonism and by compliance. Let him not cease an instant to be himself. The only joy I have in his being mine, is that the *not mine* is *mine*. . . . There must be very two, before there can be very one. Let [friendship] be an alliance of two large, formidable natures, mutually beheld, mutually feared, before yet they recognize the deep identity which beneath these disparities unites them.[62]

It remains accurate to say that Emerson is ambivalent toward Confucius's "Have no friend unlike yourself," but he is ambivalent in a new way. Whereas in "Society," he tempers his apparent agreement with the quote by conceding the probable need to lower one's criteria in order to attain the goods of friendship, Emerson now suggests the *impossibility* of having a friend unlike yourself, *as well as* the impossibility of *not* doing so. "A friend," writes Emerson, "is a sort of paradox in nature. I who alone am, I who see nothing in nature whose existence I can affirm with equal evidence to my own, behold now the semblance of my being, in all its height, variety, and curiosity, reiterated in a foreign form; so that a friend may well be reckoned the masterpiece of nature."[63]

To be sure, Emerson's description of the friend as "the masterpiece of nature" rings of exaltation. Still, the friend is conferred this distinction not because of his inestimable worth, but because he embodies a paradox, at once "the semblance of my being" and "a foreign form." Given the undulations of Emerson's attitude toward friendship, it is uneasy to surmise how we are to take this description. I think it is significant that Emerson calls the friend *the* masterpiece of nature rather than *a* masterpiece of nature. This wording suggests a singular quality of friendship. As such, the laudatory tone of the comment calls for emphasis, even if the remark is accompanied by an undertone of reticence. Such a reading is consistent with Emerson's stating, "I do not wish to treat friendships daintily, but with the roughest courage. When they are real, they are not glass threads or frostwork, but the solidest things we know."⁶⁴ *When they are real,* friendships are "the solidest things," but there is always the possibility that they will prove illusory, the stuff of "glass threads or frostwork."

It seems that Emerson's view of friendship elides the sort of questions surrounding *peng* and *you* in the Confucian tradition. In contrast to the Confucian conception of the friend–friend relationship, there is little in Emerson's thought to suggest that it is analogous to the brother–brother relationship. Given the spurts of romantic prose with which Emerson recurrently idealizes friendship, it seems more akin to a husband–wife relationship (albeit one forged in Emerson's cultural context rather than Confucius's). Consider, for instance, Emerson's remarks on the end of friendship:

> The end of friendship is a commerce the most strict and homely that can be joined; more strict than any of which we have experience. It is for aid and comfort through all the relations and passages of life and death. It is fit for serene days, and graceful gifts, and country rambles, but also for rough roads and hard fare, shipwreck, poverty, and persecution.⁶⁵

Emerson could easily have quoted from the *Book of Common Prayer*, stating that a friend is "to have and to hold from this day forward, for better for worse, for richer for poorer, in sickness and in health, to love and to cherish, until we are parted by death."⁶⁶ Friendship is thus an "an absolute running of two souls into one."⁶⁷

Elaborating on this point, Emerson credits God with using friendship as a way to dissolve barriers that would otherwise sequester disparate souls from one another:

> My friends have come to me unsought. The great God gave them to me. By oldest right, by the divine affinity of virtue with itself, I find them, or rather not I, but the Deity in me and in them derides and cancels the thick walls of individual character, relation, age, sex, circumstance, at which he usually connives, and now makes many one.⁶⁸

At this point, it would seem that Emerson would be in complete agreement with the statement from Confucius that he once rejected. "Have no friend unlike yourself" seems to be an underlying motto when Emerson describes friendship as "an absolute running of two souls into one," heralding the power of friendship to "deride" and "cancel" walls that separate individuals from one another.

Indeed, that Emerson views friendship as the "divine affinity of virtue with itself" suggests a fundamental compatibility between his notion of friendship and Confucius's. And it is this aspect of their view of friendship that I think is most crucial when considering their compatibility. I have argued that for Confucius, mutual moral cultivation is the hallmark of friendship. I have begun to show that the same is true of Emerson. References to virtue abound in "Friendship." Examining the context of some of these references will strengthen my case for compatibility with Confucian thought about friendship.

The first appearance of "virtue" in "Friendship" occurs in the midst of Emerson's discussion of the pending visit of the stranger:

> See, in any house where virtue and self-respect abide, the palpitation which the approach of a stranger causes. A commended stranger is expected and announced, and an uneasiness betwixt pleasure and pain invades all the hearts of a household. His arrival almost brings fear to the good hearts that would welcome him.[69]

Emerson suggests that a mixture of pleasure and pain overcomes the members of a house where virtue and self-respect abide. But why should the pending visit of a commended stranger cause uneasiness in the hearts of the virtuous and self-respecting? My reading is speculative, but perhaps it is their standing as praiseworthy moral agents that prompts excitement at the prospect of meeting someone else of good repute, and it is the very same aspect of their identity that causes them to worry—almost to fear—that they are not his moral equal. In short, they worry that the commended stranger is their moral superior, which might expose (to him, or to themselves) their vulnerabilities—in their own home, no less. As we have seen, during the course of his visit, the commended stranger reveals his defects, and the image that had been built of him is shown to be false. He is welcome to visit again, but the scintillation that he once aroused is not to return. There is little to be said in favor of forging a friendship with the stranger, as such a bond is lacking in the potential for growth in virtue.

Once we have found a friend, much of our satisfaction with this relationship derives from our shared virtue. On this view, virtues are not discretely possessed; they are possessions held *mutually* by both friends. Therefore, "I must feel pride in my friend's accomplishments as if they were mine,—and a property in his virtues."[70] There is an affinity between this view and that expressed in *Analects* 16.4. If my friend's virtue *is* my virtue, then it stands to reason that the beneficial types of friendship would be those that involve befriending of those who are virtuous. Confucius cites friendships with those who are upright, those who are true to their word, and those of broad learning. Numerous others could be enumerated.

Sometimes it comes to light, however, that we do not, after all, stand for the same values. Perhaps we never really did, or perhaps our friend has changed. In any case, we come to the sobering realization that our friend is not who we projected him to be. Thus, "in the golden hour of friendship, we are surprised with shades of suspicion and unbelief. We doubt that we bestow on our hero the virtues in which he shines, and afterwards worship the form to which we have ascribed this divine inhabitation."[71] We can imagine a number of permutations of friendship precipitating in this way. It is not difficult to imagine that we had been a party to one of the three types of friendship that Confucius deems harmful in *Analects* 16.4. Perhaps our friend had been a clever flatterer, a skillful dissembler, or smoothly glib. Again, other descriptions are possible.

If the viability of a friendship is measured by the quality of the friends comprising it, we should expect that Emerson would advise attentiveness to one's own character within the context of friendship. Emerson does note, "The only reward of virtue is virtue; the only way to have a friend is to be one."[72] But this is far from an expression of the importance of daily introspection about whether one has been a trustworthy friend, as we find from Master Zeng in *Analects* 1.4. Emerson appears not to give much consideration to the possibility of our own virtue being overestimated, rather than that of our friend. At the same time, Emerson identifies the problem of our being overly eager to enter into friendships, stating, "Respect so far the holy laws of this fellowship as not to prejudice its perfect flower by your impatience for its opening. We must be our own before we can be another's."[73] Moreover, once we have a friend, we should be wary of smothering him. As Emerson puts it, "Treat your friend as a spectacle. Of course he has merits that are not yours, and that you cannot honor, if you must needs hold him close to your person. Stand aside; give those merits room; let them mount and expand."[74]

There is an apparent inconsistency here, as Emerson seems to have articulated a relationship of identity between friends when it comes to virtue, yet he now refers to "merits" that only the friend has. I think there is tension between these strands of Emerson's thought on friendship, apropos of the basic instability that Emerson sees as characterizing friendship.[75] Still, we may recognize with Emerson that friends strive to "have" what is best in each other, take mutual ownership over who *they* are, and recognizing that character is not stagnant, allow their own and that of their friend to develop, recalibrating attuned to the rhythms of the relationship. Possession of virtue or character is not, of course, like the possession of an object in one's pocket. It cannot be given or taken, though it can radiate and be absorbed. Emerson suggests as much when resolving, "So I will owe to my friends this evanescent intercourse. I will receive from them, not what they have, but what they are. They shall give me that which properly they cannot give, but which emanates from them."[76]

CONCLUSION

When sharing his aspirations with his disciples in *Analects* 5.26, Confucius replies, "I would like to bring peace and contentment to the aged, to share relationships of trust and confidence with my friends, and to love and protect the young."[77] Confucius thus conceives of his personal aspirations in terms of what he can do to enhance the lives of others—all others, the aged, the young, and those in between. Presuming that Confucius intends such effects with the aged and the young via personal interactions, it may be said that each of his aspirations requires cultivating friendships.

It is difficult to say with confidence how Emerson would react to Confucius's response. He might offer the sobering reply, "The higher the style we demand of friendship, of course the less easy to establish it with flesh and blood. We walk alone in the world. Friends, such as we desire, are dreams and fables."[78] On the other hand, Emerson might admire Confucius's response, encouragingly reminding him, "The essence of friendship is entireness, a total magnanimity and trust."[79]

In the end, it is clear that Confucius and Emerson overlap significantly in their conceptions of friendship and its role in a life well lived. Each regards friendship as a context of mutual moral development, with virtue a binding agent that keeps friends together, or when absent, pulls friends apart. While Emerson regards himself as departing from Confucius's thought on friendship in "Society," it seems that he draws nearer in "Friendship." This is not to suggest that Confucius and Emerson are indistinguishable on this subject. Whereas Emerson alternates between expressions of thanksgiving and misgiving when it comes to friendship, Confucius is persistent in his avowal of its significance, its prospects, and the importance of handling it with care. Taken together, Confucius and Emerson present a robust account of the power of friendship, in spite of its fragility, to make our characters more virtuous and our lives more joyful.

2

Confucianism and Thoreau

Civil Disobedience

INTRODUCTION

While it is generally acknowledged that Asian philosophies are prominent among Henry David Thoreau's influences,[1] the interpretive literature is relatively sparing in studies of the Confucian influence upon Thoreau's thought.[2] When this influence has been acknowledged, it has tended to be marginalized. In his *The Orient in American Transcendentalism*, Arthur Christy asserts that although Thoreau took interest in Confucian texts, it is "fruitless to attempt finding in [Thoreau] a resemblance to the ethics of Confucius," that there is "nothing essentially Confucian in Thoreau's temperament," and that "no Confucius would ever have gone to Walden."[3] Likewise, in his account of "Thoreau's Quotations from the Confucian Books in *Walden*," Lyman V. Cady maintains that Thoreau "for the most part uses Confucian materials in a non-Confucian way," as "he rarely sees these sayings in their proper implications."[4] Contrary to these readings, and following Hongbo Tan, whose "Confucius at Walden Pond: Thoreau's Unpublished Confucian Translations" reveals that Thoreau engaged with Confucian ideas more than has traditionally been appreciated, I ask, "Is it Thoreau who misread Confucius? Or have Thoreau scholars all along misread Thoreau's reading of Confucius?"[5]

In his writings, Thoreau duplicates some of the quotes he and Emerson published in the "Ethnical Scriptures" column of *The Dial*, and he often gives his own English translations of excerpts from Jean-Pierre Guillaume Pauthier's French translation of the *Four Books* (1841).[6] As Tan has detailed, Thoreau translated ninety-six paragraphs from Pauthier's text in a bound notebook, interspersing notes and apparently culling passages in a "savings bank" from which he could readily withdraw ideas or quotations.[7] Tan accounts for Thoreau's use of twenty-eight of these passages, with six passages in *A Week on the Concord and Merrimack Rivers* (1849), two in "Civil Disobedience"[8] (1849), fifteen in *Walden* (1854), one in "Walking" (1861), three in the *Letters*, and a single long passage in an unpublished manuscript fragment.[9] Although Thoreau never specifies the date of his translations, because he used them in the second drafts of *A Week* and *Walden*, we can infer that they are to be dated no later than 1849.[10] This means that Thoreau could have made these translations any time between 1841 and 1849.[11]

Given its proximity to Thoreau's engagements of the Confucian texts, as well as its general renown, it is fitting that scholars who have attended to the Confucian influences on Thoreau have focused on *Walden*. In this chapter, I extend the scope of this comparative engagement to Thoreau's "Civil Disobedience."[12] I show that Thoreau's relationship to Confucius in this text is complex, for on one hand, Thoreau explicitly takes his own position concerning the relationship of citizen to government to be contrary to Confucius's, while on the other hand, his position is consistent with Confucian principles. Consequently, perhaps Thoreau's reading of Confucian texts was not *entirely* accurate, but perhaps the same is to be said of scholars' readings of Thoreau.

ANALECTS 8.13 AND *MENCIUS* 4A5

When it comes to explicit references to Confucian texts in "Civil Disobedience," Tan's tally of two is correct. The first reference is a partial quote of *Analects* 8.13, while the second is an allusion to *Mencius* 4A5.

In neither case does Thoreau appear enamored of Confucian ideas. In fact, in the first case, he immediately announces his opposition to the Confucian idea invoked:

> A man may grow rich in Turkey even, if he will be in all respects a good subject of the Turkish government. Confucius said: "If a state is governed by the principles of reason, poverty and misery are a subject of shame; if a state is not governed by the principles of reason, riches and honors are then the subjects of shame." No: until I want the protection of Massachusetts to be extended to me in some distant Southern port, where my liberty is endangered, or until I am bent solely on building up an estate at home by peaceful enterprise, I can afford to refuse allegiance to Massachusetts, and her right to my property and life. It costs me less in every sense to incur the penalty of disobedience to the State than it would to obey. I should feel as though I were worth less in that case.[13]

In refusing the right of Massachusetts to his property and life, Thoreau rejects what he regards as Confucius's notion that proper moral valuation of the fortunes of a citizen is contingent on the principles of reason by which his state is governed. Thoreau seems to read Confucius as normatively prescribing shame to the citizenry, but an alternate reading—one more compatible with Thoreau's own thought—seems plausible: if a state is governed by the principles of reason, the government ought to feel shame at the presence of poverty and misery among its people.[14]

In the second case, the common-sense nature of the idea discussed is underscored by its having found expression in (of all places!) Confucian thought: "The progress from an absolute to a limited monarchy, from a limited monarchy to a democracy, is a progress toward a true respect for the individual. Even the Chinese philosopher was wise enough to regard the individual as the basis of the empire."[15] One might expect "the Chinese philosopher" to refer to Confucius; several scholars have assumed this referent.[16] Thoreau's notebook reveals the source he had in mind is not Confucius, however, but Mencius: "Mencius said—Men have a constant way of speaking [without very well understanding it]. All say: the empire, the kingdom, the family. The basis of the empire exists in the kingdom; the basis of the kingdom exists in the family; the basis of the family exists in the person."[17]

So, we have two ideas explicitly drawn from Confucian sources, the first of which Thoreau seems to repudiate, and the second of which Thoreau seems to advocate. What can we establish from Thoreau's use of these passages? It would seem that at most we could say that Thoreau demonstrates a passing interest in Confucianism, exhibiting ambivalence with respect to these ideas. Although a reasonable conclusion to draw from what is initially apparent in the text, I believe that Thoreau engages much more with Confucianism in "Civil Disobedience" than immediately meets the eye. Furthermore, I believe that Thoreau is much more Confucian than he is aware, or than he lets on. To establish this, it will be necessary to give some explication of the text, pausing to identify possible points of engagement with Confucian ideas. I will focus my discussion of "Civil Disobedience" on two themes: problems endemic to government and problems endemic to citizens. First, however, it is necessary to gain some clarity on the essay's central concept. What *is* civil disobedience?

ON CIVIL DISOBEDIENCE

On the surface, it seems that civil disobedience is a form of disobedience that is at the same time respectful and nonaggressive (i.e., civil). The notion of a peaceful protest as a type of civil disobedience is consistent with this view. The "civil" in civil disobedience does not denote civility, however, but civil law. At its core, civil disobedience is disobedience of civil law (i.e., the codified principles governing a community, to which one is subject, barring a change in citizenship). Addressing this ambiguity, and referring explicitly to Thoreau's use of the term, Edward H. Madden and Peter H. Hare quip, "Thoreau in the earlier title of his famous essay, 'Resistance to Civil Government,' surely did not wish to imply that the American government was distinctive in its courteousness."[18] Scholars have formulated numerous sets of criteria that must be in place for an act of disobedience of civil law to constitute civil disobedience. It is beyond the scope of what is necessary for my purposes to sift through these accounts in order to locate a precise set of necessary and sufficient conditions for civil disobedience. Rather, I would like to underscore a part of the account given by Madden and Hare:

> The defiance involved in civil disobedience may take the form of doing what is prohibited or in failing to do what is required. The defiance must be a premeditated act, understood to be illegal by the perpetrator, and understood to carry prescribed penalties. Willingness to accept such penalties is a part of that sort of civil disobedience which hopes to stir the conscience of the public and the government, while eagerness to escape punishment is compatible with that sort of civil disobedience which aims to pressure the public and the government.[19]

Notice that this conception of civil disobedience leaves open the possibility of civil disobedience being violent. Madden and Hare stipulate that if civil disobedience is violent, the violence "must be planned, minimized, and controlled for maximum effectiveness in focusing the public and governmental conscience on specific injustices and/or in pressuring the government and public to change specific laws, policies, or commands (or lack thereof)."[20] This stipulation is important, as without it, a wide range of impulsive and wanton acts could be construed as civil disobedience. Violence does not enter the equation in Thoreau's described behavior in "Civil Disobedience," but the question of compatibility between Confucian thought and Thoreau's thought on the justification of civil disobedience requires that some attention be paid to this facet. As we will see, Confucius and Mencius both treated this subject explicitly.

CONFUCIANISM IN "CIVIL DISOBEDIENCE"

Much has been made of Thoreau's provocative opening of "Civil Disobedience": "I heartily accept the motto, 'That government is best which governs least,'" as well as his claim, "That government is best which governs not at all."²¹ It is common for Thoreau to be deemed, on the basis of these words, an early anarchist. We should not be quick to do so. Attending to Thoreau's own words just two paragraphs later, we find him distancing himself from "those who call themselves no-government men," stipulating that he asks for "not at once no government, *at once* a better government."²² Taking Thoreau at his word, perhaps a society with no formal governing body is a long-term goal, but the immediate goal—that with which "Civil Disobedience" is concerned—is to improve a government that he views as deeply dysfunctional.

An immediate resemblance between Confucius and Thoreau is apparent,²³ insofar as Confucius was also of the opinion that his government was deeply dysfunctional and he sought to remedy the situation. Of course, this resemblance obtains among many thinkers; it is not enough to warrant the claim that Thoreau's thought in "Civil Disobedience" is Confucian. If Confucius thought something to the effect of "that government is best which governs least," however, a case could begin to be made. I submit that this is just the sentiment expressed in *Analects* 2.3:

> The Master said, "If you try to guide the common people with coercive regulations and keep them in line with punishments, the common people will become evasive and will have no sense of shame (*chi* 道). If, however, you guide them with virtue (*de* 德), and keep them in line by means of ritual (*li* 禮), the people will have a sense of shame and will rectify themselves."²⁴

This passage is one among several in which Confucius advocates ruling through the example of virtue rather than force. It is also a passage Thoreau quotes in *Walden*, as the closing words of "The Village," although he does not offer a hint of attribution: "You who govern public affairs, what need have you to employ punishments? Love virtue, and the people will be virtuous. The virtues of a superior man are like the wind; the virtues of a common man are like the grass; the grass, when the wind passes over it, bends."²⁵ The implication is that virtue is contagious; if leaders of governments are virtuous, citizens will, in turn, be virtuous. Likewise, coercion is counterproductive. There is no doubt that coercion can instill fear in the people, but it will not inspire them to care about the flourishing of society. Compliance borne of compulsion, then, is less likely to be sustained than that which has been cultivated as part of one's character, inspired by a leader whose actions spring from a benevolent character.

The contagion of virtue is captured again in Confucius's response when asked about governing in *Analects* 12.17, "To 'govern' (*zheng* 政) means to be 'correct' (*zheng* 正). If you set an example by being correct yourself, who will dare to be incorrect?"[26] This idea is illustrated again in *Analects* 5.3, which Thoreau translated and recorded (but apparently never quoted): "The Philosopher said that Tseu-tsien (one of his disciples) was a man of a superior virtue. If the Kingdom of Lou possessed no man superior, where could this one have taken his eminent virtue? C."[27] The notion that virtue could spread from those in government to the citizenry is expressed in numerous passages in the *Analects*.[28] It is hard to imagine Thoreau failing to notice.

When rulers guide with punishments, citizens act so as to avoid punishments. When rulers guide with virtue, citizens act so as to be virtuous. These two ways of acting are not coextensive. One can act viciously, but sneakily, so as to avoid punishments. One cannot act viciously, but sneakily, so as to be virtuous! Confucius warns against the perils of a type of what we might call "authoritarian" government (recognizing that this term is not in his vocabulary), highlighting the corrosive effect that such governing has on the character of the citizenry. Here lies another similarity between Confucius and Thoreau. Thoreau grinds at least two axes in "Civil Disobedience": one against his federal government, and one against his fellow citizens. Like Confucius, Thoreau believes that authoritarian governing engenders a lack of shame in the citizenry. Instead, citizens acquiesce to actions that they know to be inhumane, fearful of the possible consequences of voicing disagreement with the government. Thoreau continually refers to the institution of slavery[29] and the waging of war against Mexico[30] (and once alludes to the treatment of Native American Indians)[31] as examples of atrocities perpetuated by the aggressive hands of the government, which have been condoned by its intimidated citizenry. Thoreau calls the Mexican-American War "the work of comparatively a few individuals using the standing government as their tool; for, in the outset, the people would not have consented to this measure."[32] So, Thoreau continues, "Governments show thus how successfully men can be imposed on, even impose on themselves, for their own advantage."[33]

That Thoreau thinks that the people "would not have consented to this measure," that the citizenry has been "imposed on, even impose on themselves," suggests that Thoreau thinks that people—even perhaps those few in government—are not naturally vicious. They become vicious as a result of anticipated gain from vicious action. This notion coheres with Confucius's claim at *Analects* 17.2, "By nature people are similar; they diverge as the result of practice." At the same time, Confucius does not elaborate on how people are similar by nature and in what way they diverge as the result of practice. His silence on this subject is deemed noteworthy in *Analects* 5.13.[34]

Rather than Confucius, then, a parallel may be more pointedly drawn with the following excerpt from *Mencius* 6A15, which Thoreau translated and recorded (but apparently never quoted):

> Koung-tou-tseu[35] put a question in these terms: All men resemble one another. Some are however great men, others little men; how so?
>
> Mencius said: If one follows the inspirations of the great parts of himself, he is a great man; if one follows the inclinations of the little parts of himself, he is a little man.
>
> Each man possesses nobleness in himself; only he does not think to seek it in himself.[36]

In short, the few in positions of leadership in government follow the inclinations of the little parts of themselves, and they influence the rest of society to do the same, discouraging them from following the inspiration of the great parts of themselves with the threat of punishment and the removal of protections that the government provides.

Even in conversing with "the freest" of his neighbors, Thoreau finds "that they cannot spare the protection of the existing government, and they dread the consequences to their property and families of disobedience to it."³⁷ "If I deny the authority of the State when it presents its tax-bill," Thoreau speculates, "it will soon take and waste all my property, and so harass me and my children without end. This is hard. This makes it impossible for a man to live honestly, and at the same time comfortably, in outward respects."³⁸ While there is something admirable about such fears from a Confucian standpoint—at least with respect to worries about the protection of one's family—Thoreau excoriates his fellow citizens for resigning their honesty to the state. This "undue respect for law" results in "a file of soldiers, colonel, captain, corporal, privates, powder-monkeys, and all, marching in admirable order over hill and dale to the wars, against their wills, ay, against their common sense and consciences, which makes it very steep marching indeed."³⁹ Referring to an individual who serves his government in violation of his conscience as "a mere shadow and reminiscence of humanity," Thoreau asserts, "The mass of men serve the state thus, not as men mainly, but as machines, with their bodies."⁴⁰ Patrick K. Dooley's summary of Thoreau's position in "Civil Disobedience" is apt: "society and the policies of the state are always subservient to the conscience of individual citizens. If a policy violates a citizen's conscience, he should disobey it."⁴¹

At this juncture it is useful to distinguish between two senses of "conscience." Some mean by conscience a voice in their heads (or their hearts, or the pits of their stomachs) that tells them what they ought to do and what they ought not to do, often in situations in which one is tempted to deviate from what one ought to do. Others mean by conscience the result of critical deliberation, considering all the relevant moral factors in a given situation. In his discussion of Thoreau's "Civil Disobedience," Peter Singer underlines this distinction and suggests that when Thoreau uses "conscience," he intends the latter sense of the word. Singer concludes that while it is easy to accept Thoreau's position, "it cannot possibly give us any guidance when we have to decide whether to obey a law," for the view "amounts only to the assertion that we should assess the rights and wrongs of obeying a law."⁴² Thinking that Thoreau offers nothing more than the truism that final decisions are up to the individual, who should base his decision on moral considerations, Singer is left wanting for an explanation as to when it is right to break the law. After all, an authoritarian could agree to all of this and suggest that the fact that an act is illegal is an overriding moral reason against doing it.[43]

Compelling as Singer's argument is, I think that he conflates legality and morality—or at least his imagined authoritarian is guilty of doing so. An authoritarian may indeed claim that the fact that an act is illegal is an overriding moral reason against doing it, but from the authoritarian, this claim begs the question. On the other hand, a citizen with no predilection for or against conforming to civil law, but rather with a predilection toward doing what is morally right, will undergo moral deliberation, exercise his critical conscience, and do what he thinks is right, even if the act should happen to be illegal. There is some resemblance between this view as it appears in "Civil Disobedience" and Confucius's insistence upon doing what is *yi* (義) (i.e., right, dutiful, appropriate). As Confucius puts the point in *Analects* 4.10, "*Junzi* in making their way in the world are neither bent on nor against anything; rather, they go with what is *yi*."[44] For an example of this principle at work, consider *Analects* 9.3:

> The Master said, "A ceremonial cap made of linen is prescribed by the rites, but these days people use silk. This is frugal, and I follow the majority. To bow before ascending the stairs is what is prescribed by the rites, but these days people bow after ascending. This is arrogant, and—though it goes against the majority—I continue to bow before ascending."

Although Confucius is not advocating breaking the law, he is advocating breaking from ritual, a rather extraordinary scenario given the premium he normally places on the rites.[45] Confucius justifies going along with the break from ritual when it comes to the fabric of the ceremonial cap, due to an overriding moral consideration; the cost of linen caps is apparently overly prohibitive. There is no suggestion that Confucius has stopped thinking ritual to be important. That he continues to don a ceremonial cap, despite the change in fabric, suggests that he thinks it important to preserve the ritual but also to be mindful that preserving ritual does not come at the cost of driving the people into poverty. There is no overriding moral consideration, however, to justify the choice of the majority to bow after ascending. Consequently, with no good reason to defy the ritual, he follows it. Ironically, he rebels against the majority in order to conform to the prescriptions of custom. In each case, his behavior is aimed at doing what is *yi*.

Thoreau continually distinguishes between men *qua* men and men *qua* machines, indicating that men are rightly described as such when characterized by moral integrity. "If the injustice is part of the necessary friction of the machine of government," he insists, "let it go, let it go . . . if it is of such a nature that it requires you to be the agent of injustice to another, then, I say, break the law. Let your life be a counter friction to stop the machine."[46] Thoreau's distinction between men in name and men in reality is reminiscent of the Confucian preoccupation with *zhengming* (正名), the "rectification of names." Confucius states his concern for *zhengming* explicitly in *Analects* 13.3 as his top priority, were he to be employed to serve in the government, and implicitly in *Analects* 12.11, when saying (in response to being questioned about governing), "Let the lord be a true lord, the ministers true ministers, the fathers true fathers, and the sons true sons." Mencius, too, emphasized this theme. Thoreau translated and recorded this excerpt from *Mencius* 6A17, another that he apparently did not quote explicitly: "What men regard as nobleness, is not true and noble nobleness. Those whom *Tchao-meng* [first minister of the king of *Thsi*] has made noble, <Thcha> *Tchao-meng* can make. <degrade> <abase>"[47] A clearer rendering would indicate that honor contingent on dispensation by others is not real honor. In his position of power, Zhao Meng can just as soon degrade those whom he has honored. His estimations of the worth of people are not necessarily accurate, and because he may encourage vice and/or discourage virtue, he distorts people's perceptions of the truly honorable.

Thoreau continually expresses frustration with the preponderance of people who are aware of the difference between justice and injustice but who convince themselves that they have done what they can to promote the former when really they only gestured in this direction. "There are thousands who are *in opinion* opposed to slavery and to the war, who yet do nothing in effect to put an end to them," Thoreau observes, chiding those who opt instead to "sit down with their hands in their pockets, and say that they know not what to do, and do nothing."[48] At most, such individuals will cast a vote for what they think is right, but they will do nothing more if their cause does not prevail. That so many do not live up to their own thoughts or voiced opinions in their concerted actions is a source of agitation for Thoreau, and indeed too for Confucius. When asked about the *junzi* in *Analects* 2.13, Confucius answers, "They first accomplish what they are going to say, and only then say it."[49] Similarly, in *Analects* 14.27, Confucius says, "The *junzi* is ashamed to have his words exceed his actions."

Thoreau certainly cannot be accused of uttering words that exceed his actions. One of the most memorable excerpts from "Civil Disobedience" is the vignette concerning his refusal to pay his poll-tax and his subsequent night of imprisonment that might have been longer had someone (most speculate it was a relative) not paid his tax for him. Thoreau recounts the experience almost nonchalantly, only expressing annoyance at the "foolishness of that institution which treated [him] as if [he] were mere flesh and blood and bones, to be locked up,"[50] thinking it more suitable to put him to work in some way. Thoreau tells of his eagerly conversing with his incarcerated roommate, fearing that he would never see him again and reading all the tracts that had been left in the prison, as well as verses that had been composed by former prisoners. In *Analects* 7.22, Confucius says, "When walking with two other people, I will always find a teacher among them." If it can be said that Thoreau "walked" with others during his short stay in prison, it seems that he abided by Confucius's practice.

ON CONFUCIAN CIVIL DISOBEDIENCE

I have yet to say whether Confucius and/or Mencius would counsel, or even condone, civil disobedience. Would they approve of breaking the law, or otherwise defying the government at the risk of, or even expecting, imprisonment or harsher punishment? I believe there is textual support in the *Analects* and the *Mencius* to answer in the affirmative, however, this response must be joined by a caveat. Neither

Confucius nor Mencius would counsel the citizenry to perform acts of civil disobedience as Thoreau envisions. Instead, under certain conditions, they would allow for ministers (i.e., those working in the service of rulers) to perform acts of civil disobedience.

A concept that is crucial to this discussion is *minben* (民本), "people as root." This term signifies the idea that the people are the foundation of the political authority of the state. Although there are disagreements concerning the origin and historical manifestations of *minben*, it is evident that Confucius and Mencius were significant promulgators of this idea. According to Viren Murthy, two claims are essential to *minben* thought: "first, the relationship between parents and children is analogous to that of rulers and masses, and second, the masses are politically passive."[51] Optimally, rulers cultivate dispositions toward the people modeled after that of nurturing parents. With their interests promoted, the people will be peaceful and harbor no inkling of revolt. The notion of *minben* is illustrated in *Analects* 13.9:

> Ranyou drove the Master's carriage on a trip to Wey. The Master remarked, "What a teeming population!" Ranyou asked, "When the people are already so numerous, what more can be done for them?" The Master said, "Make them prosperous." When the people are already prosperous," asked Ranyou, what more can be done for them?"
> "Teach them," replied the Master.[52]

Rulers should first provide the people with basic material conditions. Once this has been done, the next priority is education. The resemblance between this pair of priorities and those obligations that a parent has toward his or her child is striking.

Although we are not provided with context for Confucius's remarks at *Analects* 13.29, his comment here certainly seems connected with those of *Analects* 13.9: "The Master said, 'Having been instructed by an excellent person for seven years, the common people will be ready for anything, even the taking up of arms.'" It is noteworthy that Confucius envisions the common people being instructed by an excellent person (i.e., an instructor worthy of the designation). Not just anyone will do. Whether or not Confucius intends "seven years" as an exact figure of time is not important. Even if this is shorthand for "an extensive amount of time," the same message is conveyed. Oversight of the people requires patience and care. Once educated, the people will be prepared for "anything," including taking up arms. It should also be noted that taking up arms is not the aim of instruction. Confucius is no advocate of warfare, and he can only intend for this example to represent of the seriousness with which the people will be committed to their leaders if their leaders have gained their confidence.

The notion that leaders must gain the confidence of the people, and that their not doing so signals a moral failure, recurs throughout the *Analects*. When Duke Ding asks Confucius for a single saying that can cause a state to perish, Confucius denies that any saying can have such an effect, but he intimates that there is one saying that comes close:

> People have a saying, "I take no joy in being a ruler, except that no one dares to oppose what I say." If what the ruler says is good, and no one opposes him, is this not good? On the other hand, if what he says is not good, and no one opposes him, does this not come close to being a single saying that can cause a state to perish? (*Analects* 13.15)

Here we find clear indication of Confucius justifying opposition to government. If what the ruler says is not good, one is justified in opposing him. Indeed, if nobody does, this spells ruin for the state as a whole. In such a scenario, opposing the government is not just permissible; it is morally obligated. Moreover, it is also inevitable: "The Master said, 'When the ruler is correct, his will is put into effect without the need for official orders. When the ruler's position is not correct, he will not be obeyed no matter how many orders he issues'" (*Analects* 13.6).

The matter remains of identifying *who* is obligated to oppose government when rulers are "not good" or "incorrect." *Analects* 14.7 offers a clue: "The Master said, 'If you really care for them, can you then fail to put them to work? If you are really dutiful to him, can you then fail to instruct him?'" The first of Confucius's questions pertains to the obligations of the ruler. If the ruler is a true ruler, he ought to be able to put "them" (the people) to work, having provided basic material needs and education appropriate to the work that they are enlisted to do. The second of Confucius's questions pertains to the obligations of the minister. If the minister is a true minister, he ought to advise his lord to be a true lord.

This reading of *Analects* 14.7 is consistent with the first half of *Analects* 13.15 (of which I considered only the second half here). In the first half of the passage, Duke Ding asks Confucius for a single saying that can cause a state to flourish. Confucius replies that while there is no single saying that can have that effect, there is one that comes close: "People have a saying, 'Being a ruler is difficult, and being a minister is not easy.' If this saying helps you to understand that being a ruler is difficult, does it not come close to being a single saying that can cause a state to flourish?" Although Confucius places emphasis on the difficulty of ruling, we may even the balance by emphasizing the lack of ease associated with being a minister. The role calls for remonstrating with the ruler when the ruler acts in a way detrimental to the state. Because the ruler may think what he is doing is beneficial to the state—or may be bent on doing what he knows not to be—such remonstrations are surely difficult, but necessary.

The same position regarding rebellion against rulers is found in the thought of Mencius. Justin Tiwald describes Mencius as offering "a moral framework for members of the ruling class to instigate and sustain a revolt on the basis of the affections of the people."[53] In short, Mencius allows for ministers to rebel against rulers on behalf of the people. But he does not allow for the people to rebel against rulers. Mencius uses the parent–child analogy for the ruler–subject relation in the midst of making the latter point:

> If one is truly able to do these five things [policies of humane governance], the people of neighboring states will look to him as a father and mother and follow him like his children. Never, since the birth of humankind, has anyone ever succeeded in causing people to attack their parents. So the ruler will have no enemies in the world, and one who has no enemies in the

world is the agent of Heaven (*tian* 天). Could he then fail to become a true king? (*Mencius* 2A5)⁵⁴

As for the right of rebellion on the part of ministers, it is useful to consider what is perhaps the most notorious passage of the *Mencius*, 1B8:

> King Xuan of Qi asked, "Is it true that Tang banished Jie and King Wu assaulted *Zhou*?"
> Mencius replied, "It is so stated in the records."
> "Then can a minister be allowed to slay his ruler?"
> "One who offends against *ren* is called a brigand; one who offends against *yi* is called an outlaw. Someone who is a brigand and an outlaw is called a mere fellow. I have heard of the punishment of the mere fellow *Zhou* but never of the slaying of a ruler."

Invoking *zhengming*, Mencius denies that a king was slain by dubbing the exceptionally derelict *Zhou* "a mere fellow." A king who is a true king would not offend against both *ren* and *yi*. Having given this response to the question of whether a minister can be allowed to slay his ruler, Mencius effectively answers in the affirmative. Mencius seems to take a guarded stance in this exchange, initially offering a terse response to King Xuan's questioning. Nonetheless, Mencius does appear to suggest that a minister may be allowed to depose a ruler (or at the least, that his doing so is not tantamount to regicide, in the case of an exceptionally corrupt ruler).

Mencius's stance departs from that of Confucius in *Analects* 11.24. After his disciples, Zilu and Ran Qiu, took positions serving as ministers for the Ji family, Ji Ziran asks Confucius whether the pair can be considered great ministers. Invoking *zhengming* in his critical response, Confucius says, "What we call 'great ministers' are those who seek to serve their lord by means of the *dao*, and who resign if unable to do so. Now, Zilu and Ran Qiu are what we might call 'useful ministers.'" When asked whether they are the type who simply does what they are told, Confucius replies, "If it came to murdering their father or their lord, surely even *they* would not obey." The suggestion is that while Zilu and Ran Qiu are ineffective ministers, they are not so far gone that they would commit the most grievous of offenses.[55]

There is no indication in the *Mencius* that the people can depose a ruler, but there is clear indication that the opinion of the people in government matters (including that of deposing of others) ought to matter to the ruler:

> When those on the left and right [a ruler's close attendants] all say that someone is worthy, one should not yet believe it. When the great officers all say he is worthy, one should not yet believe it. When all the people in the state say that he is worthy, then one should investigate, and if one finds that he is worthy, only then should one employ him. . . . When those on the left and the right say, "He should be put to death," one should not yet accept it. When the great officers all say, "He should be put to death," one should not yet accept it. When all the people of the state say, "He should be put to death," one should investigate, and if one finds that he should be put to death, only then should one put him to death. Thus we have the saying, "The people of the state put him to death." By acting thus one may be able to become the father and mother of the people.[56] (*Mencius* 1B7)

In this passage, we see again the *minben* ideal of the ruler performing a role analogous to that of parent to the people. Although Murthy cites political passivity as an essential component of *minben*, this passage suggests that public sentiment carries weight with the ruler. At the same time, public sentiment is not decisive. Ultimately, "one" (the ruler) finds what he finds upon investigation.

There is evidence, then, of the permissibility of civil disobedience in the thought of Confucius and Mencius. The relationship between ruler and subject is analogous to that between parent and child and, as such, should be treated with exceptional care and humaneness. If a ruler is corrupt, the onus falls on his minister(s) to remonstrate with him. The hope is that the ruler's behavior will then be corrected, with no further conflict. If the need is dire, however, it may become appropriate for the minister to be forceful—perhaps violently forceful—against the ruler on behalf of the people.

CONCLUSION

I have just shown that there is a case to be made for the justification of some forms of civil disobedience in the thought of Confucius and Mencius. I have stipulated that any civil disobedience that Confucius and Mencius would allow would be performed by ministers, those working directly under rulers. Contra Thoreau, Confucius and Mencius would not authorize civil disobedience on the part of the citizenry. They might allow for citizens to leave for another state, however, when their own rulers are corrupt. Confucius entertains this idea in *Analects* 5.7 and imagines that his boldest disciple would accompany him: "If the *dao* is not put into practice, I will set off upon the sea in a small raft. And the one who would follow me—would it not be Zilu?"

While there is a disparity between the thought of Confucius and Mencius, on one hand, and Thoreau, on the other, there is nonetheless significant compatibility between Thoreau's thought in "Civil Disobedience" and passages that I have considered from the *Analects* and the *Mencius*. It is no surprise that Thoreau had these texts in mind at the time of the writing of the essay. Despite Thoreau's sparing and tepid explicit engagement with these texts in his essay, I think there is far more similarity than difference between Confucian views on morality and governing and those of Thoreau in "Civil Disobedience." In support of my view, I want to consider one last quote from Thoreau alongside three from the *Analects*. The first two quotes from the *Analects* are more obviously conducive to my case, while the third appears, at first blush, to be more problematic. First, Thoreau:

> I know this well, that if one thousand, if one hundred, if ten men whom I could name,—if ten *honest* men only—ay, if

one HONEST man, in this State of Massachusetts, *ceasing to hold slaves*, were actually to withdraw from this copartnership, and be locked up in the county jail therefor, it would be the abolition of slavery in America. For it matters not how small the beginning may seem to be: what is once well done is done forever.[57]

Compare Thoreau's exasperation at the elusiveness of honesty with that of Confucius at the evasiveness of *ren* in *Analects* 4.6:

The Master said, "I have yet to meet a person who truly loved *ren* or hated a lack of *ren*. . . . Is there a person who can, for the space of a single day, simply devote his efforts to *ren*? I have never met anyone whose strength was insufficient for this task. Perhaps such a person exists, but I have yet to meet him.

At the same time, compare Thoreau's optimism about the change imminently possible by one honest person with Confucius's acknowledgment, in *Analects* 7.30, of the immediacy of *ren*: "The Master said, 'Is *ren* really so far away? If I simply desire *ren*, I will find that it is already here.'" Confucius and Thoreau seem to be agreed on the rarity of an individual devoting himself to what is right, despite the potential that all people have to do so. At the same time, they are affirmative of the possibility, and hopeful of the actuality, of such individuals emerging.

It would seem that if devoting one's efforts to *ren* requires civil disobedience, Confucius and Thoreau would find all the more admirable the individual who is willing to summon the strength to do so. But a remark of Master You's in *Analects* 1.2 seems at odds with such a recommendation: "A young person who is filial (*xiao* 孝) and respectful of his elders rarely becomes the kind of person who is inclined to defy his superiors, and there has never been a case of one who is disinclined to defy his superiors stirring up rebellion." Here, "stirring up rebellion" appears to be an action that is negatively valued. It is an instance of defying of one's superiors—the kind of behavior that a filial person is disinclined toward. It should be noted, however, that Master You speaks of *inclinations*.[58] He has suggested that it is bad to be *inclined* to defy one's superiors and to be *inclined* to stir up rebellion.

At no point does Thoreau ever advocate being *inclined* to defy one's superiors or to stir up rebellion. Repeatedly, he cites as a necessary condition for civil disobedience the committing, by the government, of some great injustice. The inclination that Thoreau demands is that toward integrity of character. As I have argued, there is little evidence for thinking that this is at odds with anything that Confucius or Mencius would call for. Indeed, the balance of evidence suggests that Thoreau's call for civil disobedience is, to a significant extent, Confucian in character.

3

Confucianism and Peirce

Inquiry and Belief

INTRODUCTION

Scholars have debated the extent to which Confucius embodies a sense of authority in the *Analects*, and what, exactly, this means for the contemporary reader. The debate turns on whether Confucius is more accurately viewed as *authoritarian* or *authoritative*. "Authoritarian" denotes strict obedience to authority. Some hold that Confucius is authoritarian, a figure whose values are decidedly at odds with inquiry, independence, and innovation. The association of Confucianism with authoritarianism finds significant representation in scholarly literature. The link is clearly reflected, for instance, in the title of Shanruo Ning Zhang's recent study, *Confucianism in Contemporary Chinese Politics: An Actionable Account of Authoritarian Political Culture*.[1] Conversely, "authoritative" denotes reliability. Confucius is ordinarily viewed as authoritative when it comes to the teachings of the ancient sages and the norms of ritual practice; those who view him favorably may think him to be authoritative about much more, such as how to live a good life. Regarding Confucius as authoritarian need not exclude regarding him as authoritative in any sense, nor does regarding him as authoritative necessarily exclude him from being authoritarian. In the literature, however, the two labels stand largely in opposition. To wit, those thinking Confucius is more accurately viewed as authoritative typically dispute the notion that he is authoritarian, holding that his *not* being authoritarian is symptomatic of his authoritative comportment. This position can be inferred from the title of Sor-hoon Tan's "Authoritative Master Kong (Confucius) in an Authoritarian Age,"[2] which implies that Confucius defied cultural norms in *not* being authoritarian.

In this chapter, I will analyze Confucius's normative views concerning inquiry and belief, as portrayed in the *Analects*. I will do so through the lens of Charles Peirce's four methods of belief fixation, outlined in his essay "The Fixation of Belief" (1877). While there is not, to my knowledge, any evidence of Peirce having engaged with Confucian thought, Peirce's essay nevertheless equips us with a useful set of terms with which we can navigate this question of textual interpretation. Additionally, I will indicate how thinking through the case of Confucius as an inquirer via Peirce's vocabulary sharpens our comprehension of Peirce, recommending particular interpretations of "The Fixation of Belief" ahead of others.

DOUBT, INQUIRY, AND BELIEF

A word about Peirce's vocabulary is in order. By "fixation" of belief Peirce intends "attainment" of belief. This is clear enough when one considers his treatment of the nature of doubt and belief, immediately preceding his discussions of the four methods. Peirce describes doubt as "an uneasy and dissatisfied state from which we struggle to free ourselves and pass into the state of belief," while belief is "a calm and satisfactory state which we do not wish to avoid, or to change to a belief in anything else."[3] In fact, doubt is usually preceded by being in a state of belief—a state of belief that has proven unsatisfactory. The "uneasy and dissatisfied state" of doubt is often occasioned by a challenge to a belief; we find ourselves hesitant, surprised, or confused, in light of some experience that disrupts the certainty with which he held our belief. Inquiry is the struggle to relieve the irritation of doubt by attaining a state of belief that will not lead to further doubt: "With the doubt, therefore, the struggle begins, and with the cessation of doubt it ends. Hence, the sole object of inquiry is the settlement of opinion."[4] Peirce's four methods of fixation of belief are methods of relieving the irritation of doubt in order to achieve the settled state of belief. I will introduce and discuss these four methods shortly. First, having provided a sketch of the relationships among doubt, inquiry, and belief in Peirce's thought, it will be useful to outline the same relationships as they appear in the thought of Confucius.

Conventional wisdom has it that Confucius is the embodiment of the wise sage, imparting lessons to disciples and whoever is near. While there is some element of truth to this notion, it is woefully incomplete. In the *Analects*, Confucius is portrayed as a consummate inquirer who deems himself unmatched in his love of learning (*xue* 學),[5] and who, if granted many more years to live, would "devote fifty of them to *xue*."[6] Although *xue* often refers to the study of classical texts, for Confucius, it also includes observing and learning from others. We saw evidence of this in chapter 2, in the form of *Analects* 7.22. There, Confucius claims that when walking with two other people, he will always find a teacher among them. Inquiry is thus a principal practice of Confucius's, one that is largely situated in a social context.

Having established that Confucius places a high value on inquiry, we are left to wonder what results Confucius thinks inquiry yields. Does he, like Peirce, view inquiry as aimed at relieving the irritation of doubt? Textual evidence suggests this connection. In *Analects* 2.4, a passage that Slingerland dubs Confucius's "spiritual autobiography,"[7] Confucius purports to no longer experience doubt:

> The Master said, "At fifteen, I set my mind upon *xue*; at thirty, I took my place in society; at forty, I became free of doubts; at fifty, I understood Heaven's Mandate (*tianming* 天命); at sixty, my ear was attuned; and at seventy, I could follow my heart's desires without overstepping the bounds of propriety."

While this account of Confucius's progression from youth through various stages of adulthood is plausibly interpreted as a "spiritual autobiography," it may simultaneously be regarded as a description of epistemological development. In his youth, Confucius set his mind upon learning, and with time, the subjects of these teachings were internalized. His dispositions and behaviors harmonized with the values embodied in the teachings (perhaps *ren*, *yi*, etc.), leading to a frame of mind that was both confident and at ease. He could thus follow his inclinations, assured that however novel or difficult a circumstance, he would not veer from his *dao*.

If this interpretation has merit, *xue* may be regarded as a process of advancing from a state of doubt (or a state of many doubts) to a state that is free of doubts (and suffused with flexibility and calm). As seen in *Analects* 7.22 and 19.22, this process involves not just the study of classical texts but attentive interaction with other persons, drawn from all quarters. As such, *xue* is as much a process of discovery as it is one of mastery. This conception of *xue* overlaps with Peirce's notion of inquiry (a kind of discovering) as aimed at relieving the irritation of doubt (a kind of mastery). This resemblance between Confucius and Peirce is compelling, but it is also preliminary. Deeper affinity may be found upon considering Peirce's four methods of belief fixation.

PEIRCE'S FOUR METHODS OF BELIEF FIXATION

It is now time to turn to Peirce's four methods of belief fixation. They are: the method of tenacity, the method of authority, the *a priori* method, and the scientific method. The reader may be guided by Paula S. Rothenberg's observation: "Peirce presents the various methods of fixing belief almost as though he were giving an historical account of the necessary evolution of human beings' reasoning abilities. He treats each method as a significant advance over its predecessor so that the progression is from more to less primitive methods."[8] One should also note that in the move from one method of belief fixation to the next, the "significant advance" is both epistemic and moral.

"If the settlement of opinion is the sole object of inquiry and if belief is of the nature of a habit," Peirce writes, "why should we not attain the desired end, by taking any answer to a question, which we may fancy, and constantly reiterating it to ourselves, dwelling on all which may conduce to that belief, and learning to turn with contempt and hatred from anything which might disturb it?"[9] Such behavior characterizes the method of tenacity. Doubt quashed, belief attained and reinforced, it would seem that tenacity would be the ideal method of belief fixation. Although he identifies certain advantages to this method of belief fixation—it is "simple and direct" and "yields great peace of mind"—Peirce underscores its self-deceptive nature and regards it as the least reliable.[10] Although he would if he were fully honest with himself, "the man who adopts this method will not allow that its inconveniences are greater than its advantages."[11] As an example of the method of tenacity in action, Peirce imagines a man who "resolutely continue[s] to believe that fire would not burn him, or that he would be eternally damned if he received his *ingesta* otherwise than through a stomach-pump"[12] and likens the frame of mind of one who attains belief by the method of tenacity to that of an ostrich burying its head in the sand as danger approaches, telling itself that there is, in fact, no danger.[13]

Despite the firmness with which the tenacious individual clings to belief, Peirce believes that this method ultimately does not hold its ground. "The man who adopts it," Peirce explains, "will find that other men think differently from him, and it will be apt to occur to him in some saner moment that their opinions are quite as good as his own, and this will shake his confidence in his belief."[14] Thus, the aim of inquiry—moving from an unsettled state of doubt to a settled state of belief—is easily defeated. Because we are social creatures, we cannot rely on such an insular method of belief fixation. Ultimately, our belief will be shaken, and we will thus be unable to sustain the calmness of mind associated with belief attained by this method.

Sociality is the fulcrum upon which Peirce turns from the method of tenacity to the method of authority. Indeed, the nature of the very question of belief fixation seems to undergo a transition: "Unless we make ourselves hermits, we shall necessarily influence each other's opinions; so that the problem becomes how to fix belief, not in the individual merely, but in the community."[15] Peirce details the machinations of the method of authority at length, but these are well encapsulated in his first sentence of description: "Let an institution be created which shall have for its object to keep correct doctrines before the attention of the people, to reiterate them perpetually, and to teach them to the young; having at the same time power to prevent contrary doctrines from being taught, advocated, or expressed."[16] The method of authority thus functions much as the method of tenacity does, fending off the irritation of doubt by closing off stimuli to inquiry. The difference is that this method of belief fixation is enacted on a grand scale, with individuals resigning their faculties to the state or other institution. Although Peirce does not call the method of authority an *authoritarian* method of belief fixation, it certainly seems consistent with authoritarianism, with the state inculcating beliefs in the minds of the masses.

Although Peirce asserts that the method of authority possesses "immeasurable mental and moral superiority to the method of tenacity," his appraisal of it is far from adulatory. While Peirce points to the "most majestic results" having been borne of the method of authority (e.g., the construction of magnificent stone structures in Siam, Egypt, and Europe), he dubs those who subscribe to the method "intellectual slaves" and notes that "cruelties always accompany this system; and when it is consistently carried out, they become atrocities of the most horrible kind in the eyes of any rational man," citing the examples of tar and featherings, inquisitions, and massacres "of all who have not thought in a certain way."[17] Much like the method of tenacity, the method of authority is vulnerable to the irritation of doubt inspired by outside opinion. Inevitably, some individuals come to see that people in other countries and in other ages "have held to very different doctrines from those which they themselves have been brought up to believe; and they cannot help seeing that it is the mere accident of their having been taught as they have, and of their having been surrounded with the manners and associations they have, that has caused them to believe as they do and not far differently."[18] Virtually the same description of the inadequacy of the method of tenacity can be given for the method of authority. Because we are social creatures—aware of other social creatures (in other places and/or at other times)—we cannot rely on such an insular method of belief fixation. Ultimately, belief will be shaken, undermining the calmness of mind temporarily associated with belief attained by this method.

Recognizing that no institution can regulate all of our opinions, we may shed the method of authority and adopt what Peirce terms, following Francis Bacon, the *a priori* method. "Let the action of natural preferences be unimpeded," Peirce writes, "and under their influence let men conversing together and regarding matters in different lights, gradually develop beliefs in harmony with natural causes."[19] In other words, beliefs are arrived at through the exchange of ideas, fashioned in the mold of social taste. With this method of belief fixation, people function as rational beings in communion with one another; they are not mere subjects of an authority. At the same time, when this method is employed, one arrives at a belief consonant not with "that which agrees with experience, but that which we find ourselves inclined to believe."[20] Peirce cites as an example the widely held belief that humans act only selfishly, presuming that acting in this way, and only this way, will afford us more pleasure than acting in another. "This rests on no fact in the world," Peirce asserts, "but it has a wide acceptance as being the only reasonable theory."[21]

While Peirce deems this method of belief fixation "far more intellectual and respectable from the point of view of reason" than its predecessors, it is still deficient insofar as its making inquiry "something similar to the development of taste" renders it "more or less a matter of fashion."[22] Taste changes; fashion is fickle. As in the cases of the methods of tenacity and authority, the calmness of mind won by the *a priori* method is doomed to be temporary.

We are brought to Peirce's favored method of belief fixation, the method of science. Peirce immediately distinguishes this method from the other three by noting that with the method of science, our beliefs are "caused by nothing human, but by some external permanency."[23] Of course, it is humans attaining the beliefs in question, but they are not themselves the source of the beliefs (as in the method of tenacity), nor is the source a group in power (as in the method of authority), nor is it the drift of community (as in the *a priori* method). Whereas the other three methods placed some distance between themselves and facts, the method of science is centered on facts, or at least, the goal of uncovering them. "There are real things," Peirce explains, "whose characters are entirely independent of our opinions about them; those realities affect our senses according to regular laws, and, though our sensations are as different as our relations to the objects, yet, by taking advantage of the laws of perception, we can ascertain by reasoning how things really are."[24] Indeed, this method "must be such that the ultimate conclusion of every man shall be the same"[25] or would be the same if inquiry were sufficiently persisted in.[26] Beliefs attained via the method of science are thus more reliable than those attained via the other methods, or at least are potentially so. One learns what is more or less reliable through trial and error.

If one wishes for one's "opinions to coincide with the fact,"[27] one should choose the method of science, despite the advantages that attach to the other three methods of belief fixation. For Peirce, this is not just an epistemic matter but also a moral matter:

> But, above all, let it be considered that what is more wholesome than any particular belief is integrity of belief; and that to avoid looking into the support of any belief from a fear that it may turn out rotten is quite as immoral as it is disadvantageous. The person who confesses that there is such a thing as truth, which is distinguished from falsehood simply by this, that if acted on it should, on full consideration, carry us to the point we aim at and not astray, and then, though convinced of this, dares not know the truth and seeks to avoid it, is in a sorry state of mind, indeed.[28]

Thus, the method of science is not just the best method of belief fixation in terms of epistemic reliability[29] but also in terms of the character[30] of the believer.

In the following four sections, I will highlight passages from the *Analects* in which these methods of belief fixation are prominent. Taking seriously Peirce's underscoring of the ethical import of these classifications, I will select passages in which methods of belief fixation are tied to human conduct and character. In many cases, we witness Confucius's own methods of belief fixation. In other cases, we witness Confucius's recommendations concerning the methods used by others. Thinking through these examples will reveal several points of contact between Confucius and Peirce on the relationship between inquiry and belief.

CONFUCIUS AND THE METHOD OF TENACITY

Tim Connolly has recently suggested that Confucius's insistence upon *his dao* as *the dao* to be followed, as well as the single-mindedness apparently required to follow it, are symptomatic of Peircean tenacity.[31] In support of his view, Connolly highlights *Analects* 6.17: "The Master said, 'Who is able to leave a room without going through the door? How is it, then, that no one follows this *dao*?'" To be sure, Confucius is expressing exasperation at others' having not followed the path that he champions. Perhaps indeed Confucius sees *his* path as *the* path to be followed. Consequently, perhaps indeed a sort of single-mindedness is required to follow it. Even if this is so, Connolly's reading of this passage is unpersuasive. The conviction that one is right about something, and the determination to see it through, are not equivalent to tenacity, at least not in Peirce's sense.

Like Peirce, Confucius would find the method of tenacity least admirable as a mode of belief fixation. For Confucius, inquiry should never cease. As he puts the point in *Analects* 8.17, "Learn as if you will never catch up, and as if you feared losing what you have already attained." This remark is likely an exhortation to disciples, whose drive to persist in learning would be prone to fluctuation. The injunction to act as though afraid to lose what has already been attained should not be understood as a recommendation of tenacity when it comes to those beliefs. Rather, it should be seen as the fear of undermining one's own progress as a learner. What one has previously attained is a foundation of knowledge, skills, and character, all of which wither if one forgoes learning. Learning as if one will never catch up means to continuously fortify and build upon this foundation. Confucius's remark is an endorsement of a lifetime of inquiry. The behavior that he encourages is precisely that to which the method of tenacity is anathema.

For another passage demonstrating Confucian resistance to what Peirce calls tenacity, consider the whole of *Analects* 17.3: "Only the very wise and the very stupid do not change." One way to read this pithy remark is that the very wise (perhaps sages) have no need to change and so do not, whereas the very stupid never recognize their need to change and so do not. Given the very small number of people who would qualify as "very wise," it is likely that the remark is aimed at "the very stupid," or as a warning to those whose habits suggest such a classification. Commentators have often linked this passage with *Analects* 16.9:

> Confucius said, "Those who are born understanding it are the best; those who come to understand it through learning (*xue* 學) are second. Those who find it difficult to understand and yet persist in their studies (*xue* 學) come next. People who find it difficult to understand but do not even try to learn (*xue* 學) are the worst of all."

The "very stupid" who do not change (in *Analects* 17.3) are those in the last of the four groups described in 16.9. Learning does not come naturally to them, nor are they willing to do the difficult work of inquiry. They have thus resigned themselves to never understanding "it" (presumably, the Confucian *dao*).

Perhaps even more stupid, however, would be those who recognize their need to change but refuse to do so. Confucius addresses such cases in *Analects* 15.30, saying, "To make a mistake and yet to not change your ways—this is what is called truly making a mistake." Insisting against changing one's ways, even when recognizing the need to do so, is certainly consistent with Peirce's description of the individual whose beliefs are arrived at via the method of tenacity. Such an individual resigns his powers of critical reasoning in exchange for the security of maintaining a constant belief, no matter what its veracity might be. This habit can be morally insidious, with the individual closing himself off both from critique and the inspiring examples of others. Further elaboration is unnecessary. From these passages we can infer that Confucius would be steadfastly opposed to the method of tenacity.

CONFUCIUS AND THE METHOD OF AUTHORITY

As mentioned at the start of this chapter, scholars have debated the extent to which Confucius embodies a sense of authority in the *Analects*, with some believing that Confucius is authoritarian and others believing that he is authoritative. As we have seen, Peirce describes the perpetuator of the method of authority as keeping "correct" doctrines before the attention of the people, reiterating them perpetually, teaching them to the young, and preventing contrary doctrines from being taught, advocated, or expressed. It seems that Peirce aligns the method of authority with authoritarianism. It follows that if Confucius's methods of belief fixation (whether his own, or those he promotes to others) are consistent with Peirce's method of authority, credence will be lent to the view that Confucius is authoritarian.

Well known is Confucius's reverence for the ways of the ancient sages and for classical texts. At *Analects* 7.1, Confucius states, "I transmit rather than innovate. I trust in and love the ancient ways." At *Analects* 2.2, Confucius states, "The *Odes* (*Shijing* 詩經)[32] number several hundred, and yet can be judged with a single phrase: 'Oh, they will not lead you astray.'" It might be argued that Confucius adopts and endorses the method of authority when it comes to the ancients, whose governing practices and personal character Confucius admires and extols as exemplary.[33] It is important to recognize, however, that Confucius is not living during the time of these rulers, and that their influence has receded in his cultural landscape. Institutions of Confucius's cultural context did not promote the ways of the ancients. Promoting their ways over and against those of his contemporaries, Confucius goes against the grain. A similar analysis can be given to Confucius's exaltation of classical texts such as the *Odes* and the *Book of History* (*Shujing* 書經).[34] The rituals documented and promoted in these texts were falling out of favor at Confucius's time. Insisting on the importance of ritual propriety, Confucius defies a norm of relaxed mores.[35]

Connolly's use of *Analects* 6.17 to argue that Confucius follows the method of tenacity is perhaps more effective if redirected to argue that Confucius follows the method of authority. Although he is not himself an institution, Confucius brings his *dao* to the attention of the people, and he is primarily occupied with teaching his *dao* to the youth (his disciples). He certainly thinks this *dao* to be correct, as evidenced by his frustration at its not being followed. The question is whether Confucius prevents contrary doctrines from being taught, advocated, or expressed. Confucius does not hesitate to voice disagreement with opposing views, but this is not the same as preventing those views from being taught, advocated, or expressed. One might argue that Confucius is guilty of precisely this sort of behavior in *Analects* 17.21, in which his disciple, Zai Wo, gives a measured argument for shortening the ritual mourning period, only to have Confucius mock him to his face and criticize him after he has left. Although unremitting in his position, Confucius offers a rationale for abiding by the ritually prescribed mourning period: "A child is completely dependent upon the care of his parents for the first three years of his life—this is why the three-year mourning period is the common practice throughout the world. Did Zai Wo not receive three years of care from his parents?" It is important to note that Confucius has not prevented Zai Wo from stating his opinion, nor has he discouraged him from repeating it. Undeniably sarcastic in his endorsement, Confucius indicates to Zai Wo that if he would feel comfortable altering the mourning rituals by eating sweet foods, listening to music, and dressing comfortably, "then by all means you should!" Although Confucius is impatient with Zai Wo and undoubtedly disagrees with him, it would be difficult to argue on the basis of this passage that Confucius prevents views in opposition to his own from circulating.

Putting aside my expansion of Connolly's Peirce-inspired critique of Confucius, I want to turn briefly to what two scholars have said explicitly on the subject of Confucius and authority. Herbert Fingarette sees the *Analects* as "presenting a coherent and philosophically interesting teaching on authority-as-model,"[36] namely, that of the *junzi* as a model (hence, authoritative) human being. Fingarette's discussion prefigures that of Tan, who holds that Confucius's "teachings and conduct in the *Analects* offer an alternative model of the authoritative as an implicit critique of authoritarianism."[37] I concur with Fingarette and Tan in holding that Confucius is an *authoritative* figure, rather than an *authoritarian* one, embodying and advocating epistemic and ethical traits that his disciples would do well to cultivate in themselves. They would do well to cultivate these qualities not because they will incur some penalty if they do not (though sometimes they do indeed bear the brunt of Confucius's criticism), but because they will become better persons and citizens if they do.

Without question, Confucius exalts the *junzi* as an ideal of humanity. Numerous passages of the *Analects* feature descriptions of behaviors befitting of the *junzi*, referred to in the abstract. The following example is typical:

> The Master said, "The *junzi* is not motivated by the desire for a full belly or a comfortable abode. He is simply scrupulous in behavior and careful in speech, drawing near to those who possess the *dao* in order to be set straight by them. Surely this and nothing else is what it means to love *xue*. (*Analects* 1.14)

It is significant that although the *junzi* is a model to be followed, he is also incomplete. According to Confucius's depiction of the *junzi*, the *junzi* does not possess the *dao* but draws near to those who do in order to learn from them. Such humility, prompted not by desire for material gain but presumably by desire for intellectual and moral gain, is a true expression of the love of learning. Confucius undoubtedly wishes for his disciples to aspire to this example.

It is tempting to presume that Confucius is himself a *junzi*. Confucius directly denies that he is a *junzi*, however, stating that despite his acumen for cultural refinement, when it comes to "actually becoming a *junzi* in practice, this is something that I have not yet been able to achieve."[38] In another passage, he takes his critical self-assessment further: "How could I dare to lay claim to either sageliness or *ren*? What can be said about me is no more than this: I work at it without growing tired and encourage others without growing weary."[39]

Confucius is no despot, and his disciples constitute no mindless mass. Confucius tailors his teachings to the disciples' varying aptitudes, meeting each of them where they stand.[40] There is no hint of the method of authority at work here,[41] even if some disciples would be willing to adopt this method when in the company of Confucius. Indeed, Confucius's distaste for the notion of his disciples uncritically adopting his every belief can be inferred from the single occasion upon which Confucius faintly (and perhaps disingenuously) criticizes his best and favorite disciple, Yan Hui. Confucius asserts tersely, "Yan Hui is of no help to me—he is pleased with everything that I say."[42] This remark is rather suggestive. Although Yan Hui is likely not blindly following Confucius (he simply happens to agree with what Confucius has to say),[43] Confucius claims that Yan Hui would be of help to him if he were to part ways with him on some—any—point. Confucius wants to be challenged by his disciples, though perhaps especially by this one, whose love of learning and quality of character are most distinctive.[44] Were Yan Hui to register a disagreement with something he says, one imagines that Confucius would listen carefully, grateful to receive the thoughtful remonstration of a young intellect wise beyond his years. Certainly, Confucius would expect not to be followed were he guilty of a moral failing. As he says in *Analects* 15.36, "When it comes to being *ren*, defer to no one, not even your teacher."[45]

Peirce's description of the method of authority is more explicitly focused on institutions such as governing bodies than individual persons such as Confucius. The *Analects* provides plenty of fodder for an account of Confucius's position concerning the method of authority as instantiated in the context of the relationship between ruler and ruled. Although much of this content centers on rulers' policies and practices in governing the *behaviors* of the ruled—not the *beliefs* of the ruled, *per se*—we can nonetheless draw from these passages a Confucian position on the method of authority. At *Analects* 8.9, Confucius indicates, "The common people can be induced to travel along the *dao*, but they cannot be induced to realize it."[46] This remark may be read as indicating that while rulers may compel the common people to act in a fashion compatible with the *dao*, such conformity is more than likely little more than a façade adopted to avoid penalty. Realization of the *dao* amounts to genuine understanding of, and commitment to, the *dao*. Such understanding and commitment is not compelled externally, but comes from within.

CONFUCIUS AND THE *A PRIORI* METHOD

Recall that the *a priori* method of belief fixation involves holding fast to a socially conditioned belief or inclination, ignoring or not seeking new evidence that might undermine the belief. It is, in a way, a blend of the methods of tenacity and authority. Its distinguishing feature, that which lends it more respectability than its predecessors, is that its source is the community of which the individual believer is a member. Still, like Peirce, Confucius does not fully embrace this method of belief fixation. Confucius effectively states his opposition to such a method of belief fixation clearly in *Analects* 4.10, which we first saw in chapter 2: "*Junzi* in making their way in the world are neither bent on nor against anything; rather, they go with what is *yi*." To adopt the *a priori* method is clearly to be bent on a particular position, to have one's belief about future experience set in advance of that experience, rather than receiving new experience on its own terms.[47] Although this is not one of the several passages in which Confucius contrasts the *junzi* with the petty person (*xiaoren* 小人), one can imagine Confucius attributing the habits associated with the *a priori* method to persons of such a description.

Confucius impresses this point upon his disciples in various passages of the *Analects*. For one example, consider *Analects* 13.24:

> Zigong asked, "What would you make of a person whom everyone in the village likes?"
>
> The Master said, "I would not know what to make of him."
>
> "What about someone whom everyone in the village hates?"
>
> "I would still not know. Better this way: those in the village who are good like him, and those who are not good hate him."

Confucius acts contrary to the *a priori* method of belief fixation by resisting the impulse of "everyone" in the village. Confucius suggests that if he were going to base his opinion of the person in question upon the opinions of others, he would want for those opinions to be reliably revealing of the person's true character. The best villagers would love someone who is good and worthy of being loved, while the worst villagers would despise such a person—resentful, perhaps, for his bringing into clear relief their own defective character.[48] It might be argued that Confucius's persistent endorsement of ritual is indicative of his adopting the *a priori* method of belief fixation. Consonant with Confucius's admiring the ways of the sages, Confucius very often insists on the upholding of ritual in ceremonies and everyday behavior. Book 10 of the *Analects* is replete with descriptions of Confucius's fastidious attention to detail aligned with ritual, including the suggestion that he is attentive to ritual even in his sleep![49] It should be noted again, however, that in Confucius's context, the perceived importance of ritual was waning. Many people, and importantly, many rulers, were uninterested in preserving ritual. With this eroding of ritual, Confucius thought, came the eroding of ethics and social order. Thus, in his emphasis upon upholding ritual, Confucius is not adopting belief that conforms to social taste. On the contrary, Confucius promotes values directly opposed to those of many with whom he comes into contact.

CONFUCIUS AND THE SCIENTIFIC METHOD

We are led to the method of science, the method of belief fixation identified by Peirce as most reliable and most respectable. It is the method that supposes the reality of objective truth (as opposed to subjective opinion), and which responds to the social impulse to arrive at belief not just in the individual but also in the community. I believe there is ample evidence suggesting that Confucius's orientation toward inquiry most resembles this method. *Analects* 9.4 is important in this context, but because translations differ on at least one key phrase, it is worth considering two of them:

> There were four things the Master abstained from entirely: he did not speculate, he did not claim or demand certainty, he was not inflexible, and he was not self-absorbed. (Ames and Rosemont)

> The Master was entirely free of four faults: arbitrariness, inflexibility, rigidity, and selfishness. (Slingerland)

Confucius certainly did speculate, if by "speculate" we mean "inquire" or "wonder." Slingerland's choice of "arbitrariness" shores up this awkward piece of Ames and Rosemont's translation, as the point seems to be that Confucius faithfully abided by a standard (i.e., the *dao*). At the same time, he remained aware of his limits and those of others. These practices and dispositions betoken those of the inquirer who adopts the scientific method.

Several passages of the *Analects* further reveal Confucius's passion for inquiry, a trait that he thought important to highlight about himself, as seen previously in *Analects* 7.34:

> The Master said, "Remaining silent and yet comprehending, learning and yet never becoming tired, encouraging others and never growing weary—these are tasks that present me with no difficulty." (*Analects* 7.2)

> The Master said, "I am not someone who was born with knowledge. I simply love antiquity, and diligently look there for knowledge." (*Analects* 7.20)

> The Master said, "Do I possess wisdom? No, I do not. [For example, recently] a common fellow asked a question of me, and I came up completely empty. But I discussed the problem with him from beginning to end until we finally got to the bottom of it." (*Analects* 9.8)

That Confucius repeatedly highlights his own tirelessness in inquiry ought not to be interpreted as egoism on his part. Rather, Confucius should be viewed as teaching by example, knowing fully well that his disciples look up to him and, quite often, emulate him. The point is not to encourage their imitation *per se* but their cultivation of persistence in inquiry. Recall *Analects* 8.17: "Learn as if you will never catch up, and as if you feared losing what you have already attained."

Confucius's willingness to take seriously the question of a "common fellow" (a "simple peasant"[50] in the translation of Ames and

Rosemont) ought not to go unnoticed. For Confucius, there is no *a priori* reason to dismiss the query of a peasant; the peasant's low socioeconomic status need not indicate an impoverished intellect. Confucius denied the supposed significance of social class when it came to education, accepting disciples from all backgrounds, and seemed genuinely open to the possibility of learning from them. The case of Yan Hui, who lived in "a narrow alley, subsisting on a basket of grain and gourdful of water,"[51] exemplifies these points. Confucius's passion for learning from others is amplified in *Analects* 19.22. In this passage, Zigong is asked from whom Confucius acquired his learning. Zigong responds, in part, "From whom did the Master *not* acquire his learning?" The suggestion is that Confucius gleaned insights from virtually everyone with whom he came into contact. Assuredly, not everyone with whom he interacted yielded a markedly fruitful insight, but even the most ordinary interactions contribute to one's perceptions of others and the world.

Recall once more *Analects* 7.22: "When walking with two other people, I will always find a teacher among them. I focus on those who are good and seek to emulate them, and focus on those who are bad in order to be reminded of what needs to be changed in myself." The second sentence quoted illuminates an additional important feature of Confucius's habits of inquiry. The pursuit of knowledge is not simply about uncovering facts; it is about cultivating character. One misses opportunities of self-cultivation and growth when one refuses to undergo inquiry, no matter whether that refusal is due to self-absorbed tenacity, fearful compliance with authority, or comfortable meshing with the majority. Moreover, one misses opportunities of self-cultivation and growth when one rigidly marks off boundaries between those who are worthy of engaging in inquiry and those who are not, particularly if those boundaries are arbitrary or otherwise untenable.[52]

Harmony (*he* 和) may be seen as playing a vital role in a Confucian version of the scientific method. As Angle points out, early mentions of this term "tended to be in culinary or musical contexts, or at least to draw metaphorically on these frameworks."[53] When various notes or ingredients are blended such that their combination produces a pleasing effect, harmony is achieved. As in the cases of a musical arrangement or a soup, achieving such harmony is a matter of balance. No one instrument or ingredient should overwhelm the rest. Confucius's description of music is illustrative:

> The Master was discussing music with the Grand Music Master of Lu. He said, "What can be known about music is this: when it first begins, it resounds with a confusing variety of notes, but as it unfolds, these notes are reconciled by means of harmony, brought into tension by means of counterpoint, and finally woven together into a seamless whole. It is in this way that music reaches its perfection." (*Analects* 3.23)

This description of the process of music bears striking resemblance to that of the method of science. Competing hypotheses might be viewed as "a confusing variety of notes," experiment and testing as the nuanced process of "unfolding," with the eventual drawing of conclusions as the "weaving together into a seamless whole."

Confucius assigns harmony more than aesthetic value, stating in *Analects* 13.23, "The *junzi* harmonizes, and does not merely agree. The *xiaoren* agrees, but he does not harmonize." Following the trajectory of Peirce's methods of fixation, the *junzi* harmonizes rather than striking the same chord repeatedly, drowning out the sounds of all others (as in the method of tenacity); he harmonizes by active participation, rather than deferring to others with more power (as in the method of authority); he harmonizes by use of improvisation, rather than adhering to scripted performance (as in the *a priori* method). Committed to *xue*, not solely for his own good, but for that of others, he stays attuned to the world around him, never blocking the way of inquiry.[54]

CONCLUSION

It is usually presumed that Peirce's intent in "The Fixation of Belief" is to demonstrate that tenacity, authority, and *a priori* reasoning are inferior to the scientific method. I concur with T. L. Short, who writes, "And one would not be wrong in saying this, and yet it is a misleading statement, in two ways."⁵⁵ First, this statement is misleading because it seems to imply that Peirce applied a stable criterion against which the adequacy of the methods could be judged. Second, this statement is misleading because it assumes that Peirce makes an argument to show that the first three methods fail to meet that criterion as well as the scientific method does. According to Short, the expectation that Peirce offers an argument in "The Fixation of Belief" is unwarranted:

> Peirce did not give us reasons to agree with him. Instead, he referred to the experience of using the methods in question. The only way to follow Peirce's "argument," if we are to call it that, is to imagine having the experiences he described and confirming that they would lead us, too, to reject the methods in question.⁵⁶

Apropos of his claims in "The Fixation of Belief," Peirce intends for the reader to undergo inquiry on his own, coming to settle on the belief that the scientific method is the superior method, both epistemically and morally.

I have highlighted as characteristic of Confucius this very same intertwining of the epistemic and moral when it comes to inquiry and belief. Confucius's self-descriptions frequently underscore his twin commitments to *xue* and the *dao*. Although he regards himself as a moral work in progress, denying that he is a *junzi* and that he is *ren*, he does not hesitate to recognize his perseverance in inquiry. He does not settle on beliefs by force of habit (as in the method of tenacity), nor does he defer to the authority of others (as in the method of authority),⁵⁷ nor does he conform to the currents of popular taste (as in the *a priori* method). His method is one of patient, persistence, and gradual self-cultivation:

> The Master said, "[The task of self-cultivation] might be compared to the task of building up a mountain: if I stop even one basketful of earth short of completion, then I have stopped completely. It might also be compared to the task of leveling ground: even if I have only dumped a single basketful of earth, at least I am moving forward." (*Analects* 9.19)

Is this not the spirit of Peirce's ideal inquirer, whose inclination toward one method of belief fixation gives way to the next, culminating finally in the scientific method? One envisions the movements from tenacity to authority, from authority to *a priori*, from *a priori* to scientific method, as so many basketfuls of earth in the building up of a mountain, where the mountain is symbolic of the character of the inquirer.

As the essay draws to a close, Peirce declares, "above all, let it be considered that what is more wholesome than any particular belief is integrity of belief."[58] It seems that Confucius and Peirce would agree that such integrity is as vital as it is rare—and worthy of the dogged persistence and arduous effort requisite to its attainment. Such a view would not smack of authoritarianism but would rightly be regarded as authoritative.

4

Confucianism and James

Human Nature and Morality

INTRODUCTION

In *Analects* 5.13, we are told, "one does not get to hear the Master expounding upon the subjects of human nature (*xing* 性) or the Way of Heaven (*tiandao* 天道)." In actuality, one does get to hear Confucius discuss these subjects, although appearances of these concepts in the *Analects* are certainly scantier than other themes. My focus in this chapter is on the former term. More conspicuously absent from the text, *xing* (性) appears only one other time, at *Analects* 17.2: "By *xing* (性) people are similar; they diverge as the result of practice." With this being the entirety of the passage, we are left wanting to know in what way people are similar and how they diverge as the result of practice. Is human nature fundamentally good? Bad? Neutral? Mixed? According to Slingerland, "the lack of theoretical consistency in the *Analects* makes it possible to argue for any of these positions."[1]

The lack of a neatly identifiable Confucian position about human nature may have been a motivation for Mencius, who on many occasions argues that human nature is fundamentally good. In turn, Xunzi explicitly disagrees with Mencius, identifying his view as mistaken and arguing that human nature is bad. Drawing explicitly on a distinction coined by William James, Fung Yu-lan classifies Mencius as belonging to the "tender-minded" group of philosophers and Xunzi as belonging to the "tough-minded" school.[2] Although it would appear that they are diametrically opposed to one another, scholars are divided on the degree to which Mencius and Xunzi actually hold opposing views. I will take up a number of salient passages from the *Mencius* and the *Xunzi* in order to achieve as clear a picture as possible of where they stand on this issue.

Allusions to human nature abound across James's corpus, especially in texts focused on psychology and morality. One finds "human nature" referred to with frequency in *Principles of Psychology* (1890), *The Will to Believe and Other Essays in Popular Philosophy* (1897), and *Talks to Teachers on Psychology and to Students on Some of Life's Ideals* (1899). The subtitle of *The Varieties of Religious Experience* (1902) is "A Study in Human Nature." Still, James never offered a systematic account of human nature. It is by no means obvious how James would answer the questions that Confucius leaves unanswered. Is human nature fundamentally good? Bad? Neutral? Mixed? Considering passages of his texts after considering the *Mencius* and the *Xunzi* can help to achieve clarity on James's position.

MENCIUS AND XUNZI ON HUMAN NATURE AND MORALITY

Before considering what Mencius and Xunzi say about *xing*, it is necessary to say a word about *xing*. While Slingerland renders *xing* "human nature," this would be a more appropriate translation for *ren xing* (人性). On its own, *xing* does not mean "human nature," but something more general (i.e., "a thing's nature"). Ames and Rosemont choose "natural disposition" in *Analects* 5.13 and "natural tendencies" in *Analects* 17.2. Paul Rakita Goldin argues that Mencius and Xunzi use *xing* in two different ways, such that their claims about *xing* ought to be taken as their talking about two different things, rather than disagreeing about the same thing. For Mencius, *xing* "represents the natural course of development which an organism may be expected to undergo given nourishing conditions,"³ while for Xunzi, *xing* is far more nuanced:

> *Xing* is what we have from birth—in other words, different forms of desire. These desires are not merely appetitive; to Xunzi, human beings desire virtually everything, and engage in all manner of unscrupulous conduct in order to gain satisfaction of their desires. To our *xing* belong our senses and our faculties. *Xing* encompasses everything which we possess without having exerted any effort to obtain it.⁴

As we will see in more detail shortly, for Mencius, a person's *xing* is to be moral. For Xunzi, a person's *xing* is just what he holds in common with all other persons.

When Mencius says that human nature is good (*shan* 善), what does he mean? In fact, his disciple, Gongduzi, asks him this very question. Mencius responds:

> One's natural tendencies enable one to do good; this is what I mean by human nature being good. When one does what is not good, it is not the fault of one's native capacities. The mind of pity and commiseration is possessed by all human beings; the mind of shame and dislike is possessed by all human beings; the mind of respectfulness and reverence is possessed by all human beings; and the mind that knows right and wrong is wisdom. Humaneness, rightness, propriety, and wisdom are not infused into us from without. We definitely possess them. It is just that we do not think about it, that is all. Therefore it is said, "Seek and you will get it; let go and you will lose it." That some differ from others by as much as twice, or five times, or an incalculable order of magnitude is because there are those who are unable fully to develop their capabilities. (*Mencius* 6A6)

It is clear that Mencius does not deny that people act badly. He explains bad behavior in terms of aberration from natural tendency. Our natural tendency is in the direction of humaneness (*ren*), rightness (*yi*) propriety (*li*), and wisdom (*zhi* 智). Sometimes we "let go" and allow ourselves to act in a way contrary to our natural tendency. This is not the fault of our native capacities *themselves* but is explainable by whatever has caused our being unable to fully develop our capacities. Thus, it is no contradiction that a person's *xing* is good, but not all persons are good.

Mencius often uses agricultural metaphors in discussing the tendency of human nature toward goodness.[5] The four tendencies referenced earlier are likened to sprouts in *Mencius* 2A6:

> The mind's feeling of pity and compassion is the sprout of *ren*; the mind's feeling of shame and aversion is the sprout of *yi*; the mind's feeling of modesty and compliance is the sprout of *li*; and the mind's sense of right and wrong is the sprout of *zhi*. Human beings have these four sprouts just as they have four limbs. For one to have these four sprouts and yet to say of oneself that one is unable to fulfill them is to injure oneself, while to say that one's ruler is unable to fulfill them is to injure one's ruler.

The sprout metaphor captures Mencius's notion that these good qualities are incipient in humans. The claim that anyone is unable to develop these qualities is, strictly speaking, false. We all have the ability to develop these qualities. We shortchange ourselves if we suggest otherwise about ourselves, and we slight our ruler if we think otherwise of him.[6]

Conditions may arise, however, that frustrate or thwart our development of these qualities. Our moral development is at least in part a product of our environment. In *Mencius* 6A7, Mencius states, "In years of abundance, most of the young people have the wherewithal to be good, while in years of adversity, most of them become violent." This is not a difference in native capacities, Mencius explains, but a difference in what overwhelms the minds of the young people. Scarcity of resources impinges upon their moral sense, curbing inclinations toward *ren*, for instance, in favor of a more self-centered orientation.

Sometimes conditions are such that one's moral sense is virtually extinguished:

> Mencius said, "The king's lack of *zhi* is hardly surprising. Take something that is the easiest thing in the world to grow. Expose it to heat for a day, and then expose it to cold for ten days. It will not be able to grow. I see the king but seldom, and when I withdraw, the agents of cold arrive. Even if I have caused some buds to appear, what good does it do?" (*Mencius* 6A9)

Mencius indicates that the growth of the king's *zhi* has been stunted by "the agents of cold"—perhaps the king's inner circle of ministers and other followers who encourage despicable behavior and/or discourage good behavior. Were the king to more frequently interact with Mencius or other agents of positive influence, his natural tendencies toward the good would be nurtured, like heat helps to nurture a plant. Without such influence, and with opposing forces steadily in tow, moral development flowering to anything greater than "some buds" is impossible.

Whereas Mencius holds that human nature is fundamentally good, Xunzi makes a very different claim:

> Man's nature is evil; goodness is the result of conscious activity. The nature of man is such that he is born with a fondness for profit. If he indulges this fondness, it will lead him into wrangling and strife, and all sense of courtesy and humility will disappear. He is born with feelings of envy and hate, and if he indulges these, they will lead him into violence and crime, and all sense of loyalty and good faith will disappear. (*Xunzi* §23, 161)

Remembering that Xunzi's use of *xing* differs in sense from Mencius's use of *xing*, this passage does not bring to the foreground the critical difference between Mencius and Xunzi. Although Mencius usually emphasizes the good—that is, the four sprouts—as we saw in chapter

2, he also acknowledges, "Those who follow the part of themselves that is great become great persons, while those who follow the part that is small become small persons" (*Mencius* 6A15). There is no reason to think that Mencius would deny the conditional ("if . . .") statements issued by Xunzi in the previous passage. In fact, there is textual warrant for thinking that he would unreservedly concur.

Just as Mencius does not deny that humans act badly, Xunzi does not deny that humans act well. Like Mencius, Xunzi is making a claim about our natural tendency. His view is that our natural tendency is not toward goodness, but toward what Watson here translates as "evil" (*e* 惡). I favor the softer term, "badness," although this too may not be the best choice. It seems that Xunzi's claim is that our natural inclination is not badness *per se*, but something more akin to self-centeredness with indifference to others. According to Xunzi, "all men in the world, past and present" agree in defining *e* as "that which is prejudiced, irresponsible, and chaotic."[7]

In this context, "profit" need not be confined to material profit; to say that we are born with a fondness for profit means just that we are fond of gain, of self-benefit. To say that we are born with feelings of envy and hate just means that we naturally manifest these feelings when others gain or benefit and we do not. That goodness is the result of "conscious activity" suggests that our acting morally comes from our curbing our natural inclination toward not doing so. Morality, particularly of the other-centered kind (e.g., *ren*) is the result of deliberate effort to harness our default disposition toward selfishness.

Whereas Mencius employs agricultural metaphors for moral development, Xunzi enlists metaphors related to manual labor:

> A warped piece of wood must wait until it has been laid against the straightening board, steamed, and forced into shape before it can become straight; a piece of blunt metal must wait until it has been whetted on a grindstone before it can become sharp. Similarly, since man's nature is evil, it must wait for the instructions of a teacher before it can become upright, and for the guidance of ritual principles before it can become orderly. (*Xunzi* §23, 162)

The difference in choice of metaphor is highly illuminating. While Mencius regards the project of moral development as one of providing the nutrients needed to carefully draw out what is already there in germ, Xunzi regards the project of moral development as one of aggressively restructuring what is present from something corrupt into something viable. By no means does Mencius think that we start off *junzi*, but where he has us starting the project of moral development is substantially ahead of where Xunzi has us starting. We are born inclined toward goodness on Mencius's view of human nature, while we are born inclined against it on Xunzi's view. This summary from Donald J. Munro is apt:

> Mencius would maintain that certain innate tendencies necessarily lead to the practice of certain moral acts, and that the evaluating mind simply directs these tendencies properly. Hsün Tzu [Xunzi] would not hold that the moral acts are *direct* manifestations of innate tendencies; the mind evaluates, but the behavioral drive is not so close to the surface.[8]

The behavioral drive might very well be far from the surface, if the requisite effort to do what is good is markedly significant. Mencius has no problem explaining how a person might desire to be good; it is consistent with our *xing*. On the other hand, if our *xing* is not good, as Xunzi believes, how could we want to become good? Xunzi holds that every person who desires to do good does so precisely because his nature is bad. "Whatever a man lacks in himself," Xunzi avers, "he will seek outside. . . . What a man already possesses in himself he will not bother to look for outside. From this we can see that men desire to do good precisely because their nature is evil."[9] The majority of commentators regard this argument as ineffectual, with Goldin remarking of it that it is a road "best left untraveled."[10] If it is our *xing* to desire what we lack, and we lack goodness, it would not seem unreasonable to claim that our *xing* includes the desire to be good.

Xunzi offers a second explanation as to how we come to desire being good, which commentators are agreed is more convincing than the first:

> ... in ancient times the sages, realizing that man's nature is evil, that it is prejudiced and not upright, irresponsible and lacking in order, for this reason established the authority of the ruler to control it, elucidated ritual principles to transform it, set up laws and standards to correct it, and meted out strict punishments to restrain it. As a result, all the world achieved order and conformed to goodness. (*Xunzi* §23, 166–167)

In short, we come to see that it is in our best interest to be good. Because our *xing* is not goodness, without any sort of regulations in place, nobody can be trusted to be good. For this reason, rituals and laws must be put in place. The ruler enforces the rituals and laws, providing negative incentives associated with transgressing them. Because we want to avoid the harms of punishment, we suppress our antisocial and anarchic tendencies and strive toward goodness and order.

There is nothing sardonic about Xunzi's discussion of human nature and morality. He does not decry the institutions of ritual and law as artificial constructs that impede the natural unfolding of human behavior.[11] On the contrary, Xunzi regards these institutions as essential to sustaining societies. Xunzi opens a discussion of ritual with these words:

> What is the origin of ritual? I reply: man is born with desires. If his desires are not satisfied for him, he cannot but seeks some means to satisfy them himself. If there are no limits and degrees to his seeking, then he will inevitably fall to wrangling with other men. From wrangling comes disorder and from disorder comes exhaustion. The ancient kings hated such disorder, and therefore they established ritual principles in order to curb it, to train men's desires and to provide for their satisfaction. They saw to it that desires did not overextend the means for their satisfaction, and material goods did not fall short of what was desired. Thus both desires and goods were looked after and satisfied. This is the origin of rites. (*Xunzi* §19, 93)

It is significant that Xunzi says that both desires and goods were looked after and satisfied. If one concentrates upon fulfilling ritual principles, Xunzi asserts, "then he may satisfy both his human desires and the demands of ritual; but if he concentrates only upon fulfilling his desires, he will end by satisfying neither."[12] Simultaneously apparent in these words are the logically warranted bifurcation of *xing* and *li* and the practically demanded inextricable tie between them. While Mencius believes that the incipient four sprouts offer moral direction, Xunzi finds no innate direction toward the moral. As David B. Wong observes, Xunzi strongly emphasizes rituals because they "are especially effective in shaping and channeling human feeling." In fact, rituals "regulate and partially define occasions on which human beings have strong feelings of the sort that can become moral feelings."[13]

One might now ask whether the ancient kings chose the *li* because the *li* are good or the *li* are good because the ancient kings chose them. Addressing this dilemma, Goldin argues that "there are rituals that are right, and pretender rituals that are wrong. The proper rituals were established by the sage-kings and are proper because they conform to *human nature*."[14] Xunzi describes the three bases of rituals:

> Heaven and earth are the basis of life, the ancestors are the basis of the family, and rulers and teachers are the basis of order. If there were no Heaven and earth, how could man be born? If there were no ancestors, how would the family come into being? If there were no rulers and teachers, how would order be brought about? If even one of these were lacking, there would be no safety for man. Therefore rites serve Heaven above and earth below, honor the ancestors, and exalt rulers and teachers. These are the three bases of rites. (*Xunzi* §19, 95)

Thus, the sage-kings were not inventors; in their promotion of *li*, they expressed what is natural to humans and their place within the universe.

The difference between Mencius and Xunzi may be summarized in this way. Mencius thinks the source of morality to be internal; it is our nature to be good. Xunzi thinks the source of morality to be external; it is not in our nature to be good, so a desire to be good must be inspired in us by an outside source. One must become convinced that it is against one's interest to not be moral, and in one's interest to be moral. Recognizing that everyone's nature is like one's own (i.e., not good) leads one to accept ritual and laws as regulating forces over one's character and conduct. These rituals and laws are not arbitrary. The sage-kings enacted particular rituals and laws, regarding them as reflective of the path humans need to chart in the process of moral cultivation.

Although they make use of different styles of metaphor to express the point, both Mencius and Xunzi would agree that the process of moral cultivation is not undergone in an instant. It requires hard work and commitment, no matter whether those efforts are more akin to those of the farmer nurturing sprouts or the artisan imposing order on raw materials. In emphasizing the compatibility of their accounts, we might side with A. S. Cua, who suggests that the positions of Mencius and Xunzi are complementary, insofar as they focus upon two aspects of moral experience. Mencius sees the basic task of morality as providing *conditions of ideal achievement*, and Xunzi sees the basic task of morality as providing *conditions of restraint*.[15] Meanwhile, precisely this difference between Mencius and Xunzi may lead us to conclude with Goldin, "There is little potential for reconciliation between Mencius and Xunzi, for they disagree explicitly on how human beings will behave in their savage or pristine state."[16] My aim has not been to adjudicate among competing claims concerning the degree to which Mencius and Xunzi agree or disagree. Rather, I hope to have given clear expositions of the thought of each on the relationship between human nature and morality. If I have succeeded in doing so, my analysis of this aspect of William James's thought will be fruitful.

JAMES ON HUMAN NATURE AND MORALITY

In his incisive study of human nature in American thought, Merle Curti says of James that his references to human nature "were casual and incidental, as if of course everyone understood what was meant."[17] In fact, it is not altogether clear that James ever isolated a single conception of human nature, inasmuch as he uses the term in a wide variety of contexts and appears at times to give it contradictory characterizations. This may be telling of how James conceived of human nature—it is complex and marked by internal tensions, if not indeed contradictions. James would not be the least bit perturbed by the fact that Mencius and Xunzi could each mean something different by *xing*, nor would he be flummoxed by the notion that a being whose *xing* is good could act badly and a being whose *xing* is bad could act morally. James was attracted to seeming contradictions, as evidenced by titles of his works such as "The Sentiment of Rationality" (1882) and *A Pluralistic Universe* (1909). As Curti puts it, "He preferred to leave paradoxes dangling rather than to resolve them in misleading oversimplifications."[18] Nonetheless, there is enough in common across various comments of James's on human nature to give an intelligible account of James's notion of how human nature and morality are interrelated. Drawing on vocabulary and ideas from the thought of Mencius and Xunzi will facilitate this effort in the sections that follow.

THE HEALTHY-MINDED AND THE SICK-SOULED

Although the subtitle of *The Varieties of Religious Experience* is "A Study in Human Nature," James's treatment of various kinds of religious experience is not intended as an exhaustive description of human nature. All the same, James describes some basic features of human nature that are brought into relief by the accounts of subjects whose religious experiences he recounts in the pages of the text. For example, James observes two opposed tendencies of personality, which he labels the healthy-minded and the sick-souled. Healthy-mindedness is "the tendency which looks on all things and sees that they are good,"[19] while the sick soul is of the view that "the evil aspects of our life are of its very essence."[20] In short, the healthy-minded tendency is optimistic while the tendency of the sick soul is pessimistic. On the face of it, were James to analyze Mencius and Xunzi, he would dub Mencius a healthy-minded individual and Xunzi a sick soul, inasmuch as Mencius is much more optimistic about the inherent moral quality of human nature than is Xunzi.

Of course, Xunzi's negative outlook on *xing* does not entail that humans are ineluctably bad. There is a healthy-minded quality to Xunzi's belief that all humans have the potential to do the hard work of moral cultivation. The sick soul clings to the radical belief that "no alteration of the environment, or any superficial rearrangement of the inner self, can cure"[21] the wrongness or vice of his essential nature. Only a supernatural remedy will suffice to soften the pessimism of the sick soul and steer his temperament closer to the healthy-minded individual. This is clearly a brand of pessimism that is stronger than that of Xunzi, who does not invoke the supernatural as a necessary condition for goodness, let alone for belief in the possibility of goodness.

Because Xunzi is not thoroughgoing in his pessimism but believes in the capabilities of humans to be good, it is reasonable to resist the *prima facie* notion that Xunzi would be classified as a "sick soul." Still, James would appreciate the difference between Mencius's and Xunzi's temperaments, distinguishing as he does between involuntary and voluntary modes of healthy-mindedness. "In its involuntary variety," James explains, "healthy-mindedness is a way of feeling happy about things immediately," while voluntary (or "systematic") healthy-mindedness requires conscious effort; it "excludes evil from its field of vision."[22] According to James, the systematic cultivation of healthy-mindedness is "consonant with important currents in human nature. . . . In fact, we all do cultivate it more or less, even when our professed theology should in consistency forbid it."[23] James points to our diverting our attention from disease, death, and slaughterhouses as evidence of our striving to avoid miring ourselves in the mood of the sick soul, choosing to view the world through rosier lenses, believing that despite its pockmarks it is on the whole a place of promise and beauty. On James's distinction, Mencius seems more on the side of the involuntarily healthy-minded, given his belief in *xing* being fundamentally good, while Xunzi is more on the side of the voluntarily healthy-minded, given his belief that in order to be good, humans must (to use James's phrase) exclude evil from our field of vision, placing moral action at the forefront.

There is an interesting confluence of the metaphors of Mencius and Xunzi in the words of New Thought author Henry Wood, whom James quotes as saying,

> High, healthful, pure thinking can be encouraged, promoted, and strengthened. Its current can be turned upon great ideals until it forms a habit and wears a channel. By means of such discipline the mental horizon can be flooded with the sunshine of beauty, wholeness, and harmony. To inaugurate pure and lofty thinking may at first seem difficult, even almost mechanical, but perseverance will at length render it easy, then pleasant, and finally delightful.[24]

Flooding one's mental horizon with sunshine is reminiscent of Mencius's way of talking about cultivating the incipient sprouts of human nature, while turning the current to form a habit and wear a channel is evocative of Xunzi's way of talking about the strenuous task of ingraining morality into human nature. James's discussions of the healthy-minded and the sick soul are thus interestingly related to Mencius's and Xunzi's discussions of *xing*. Ultimately, it seems James would classify each as healthy-minded, though Xunzi's healthy-minded nature is one acquired through voluntary effort, in much the same way that he thinks human morality must be.

HUMAN NATURE, VIOLENCE, AND PEACE

Curti provides the following summary of James's nuanced position concerning the nature of habit: "James stresses the binding character of habits while opening the way to the possibility of developing new ones by the exercise of attention, choice, will, and persistent repetition."[25] This description is mostly correct, but it warrants some refining. Curti seems to imply that James thinks that once one has a habit, one has it for life. So, if one wants to cease acting in a way consonant with one's habit, one cannot omit the habit; all that one can do is develop a new habit or two that counteract the original habit. Ever the embracer of apparent (or indisputable!) contradiction, James thinks *both* that habits are binding *and* that habits are revisable. These strands of his thought are intertwined, and together they inform much of his thought about the relationship among human nature, violence, and peace. I will consider several excerpts of his writing in order to demonstrate this, and I will consider the question of whether James's thought about human nature, violence, and peace aligns him more with Mencius or with Xunzi.

James's most widely known writing concerning these subjects is the essay "The Moral Equivalent of War" (1910). In this essay, James proposes that, as an alternative to humans waging war with one another, they wage a war against nature:

> If now—and this is my idea—there were, instead of military conscription a conscription of the whole youthful population to form for a certain number of years a part of the army enlisted against *Nature*, the injustice would tend to be evened out, and numerous other goods to the commonwealth would follow.[26]

This suggestion is part and parcel of James's "moral equivalent" of war. More apt than "equivalent" would be "substitute," as James intends not to promote a *moral war* (whatever that would amount to) but rather to promote activity that is *warlike* but *moral* (i.e., does no harm to fellow humans).[27] James wishes to preserve the martial virtues that are promoted by war while avoiding the destructiveness of armed combat.

What does James have in mind by a war against nature? He describes the duties of the conscribed youth in detail:

> To coal and iron mines, to freight trains, to fishing fleets in December, to dish-washing, clothes-washing, and window-washing, to road-building and tunnel-making, to foundries and stoke-holes, and to the frames of skyscrapers, would our gilded youths be drafted off, according to their choice, to get

the childishness knocked out of them, and to come back into society with healthier sympathies and soberer ideas. They would have paid their blood-tax, done their own part in the immemorial human warfare against nature; they would tread the earth more proudly, the women would value them more highly, they would be better fathers and teachers of the following generation.[28]

The youthful army enlisted against nature would, in fact, be an army working *in* and *with* nature, albeit at times for the sake of maintaining control over nature. Energy normally expended as acts of wanton *de*struction in armed combat would be sublimated in acts of *con*struction in the "moral equivalent." Moreover, the constructive effect would be both material and moral; the enlisted (males) would develop into responsible young adults (men), who would make a positive impact on future youth.

One might question why James clings to the rhetoric of combat, devising a "moral equivalent" of war rather than proposing a paradigm shift away from war altogether. "History is a bath of blood," James writes, and "at the present day . . . military instincts and ideals are as strong as ever."[29] Citing a long-standing human proclivity toward looting, plundering, and killing, James avers, "Our ancestors have bred pugnacity into our bone and marrow, and thousands of years of peace won't breed it out of us."[30] James's "moral equivalent" of war is a concession to what he sees as a deeply grounded feature of human nature. For James, the instinct of pugnacity is an intractable part of the human condition; the question is how pugnacity shall find expression. Armed combat is one way of manifesting pugnacity, but it is by no means the only way. Whereas the former manifestation of pugnacity engenders barbarism, conquering, and bloodshed, James's proposal promotes patient endurance and productive labor.

Recalling Mencius and Xunzi, there is little question of whose description of human nature James seems to echo when discussing pugnacity. There is no hint here of Mencius's notion that human nature is fundamentally good. Rather, James exclusively emphasizes the propensity toward conflict endemic to all humans, just as Xunzi does before him. While James asserts that it is possible that armed combat could be put to an end, he stipulates that this can happen only via a rechanneling of the martial instincts. It is unavoidable that we will be at war; we simply have to choose the less deleterious types of war, the kinds that involve battles aimed at helping humanity rather than destroying some sector of humanity. This is a tall order, involving a good deal of demanding effort. The artisanal metaphors that Xunzi employs in describing the difficult process of curbing our naturally bad or self-centered behavior are made literal by James as manual labor to be undergone by youth to harness their natural pugnacity and contribute productively to society.

Xunzi and James both place emphasis on what James dubs in "The Moral Philosopher and the Moral Life" (1891) the "strenuous moral mood," an orientation toward the difficult work of attaining "higher fidelities, like justice, truth or freedom."[31] According to James, "The capacity for the strenuous mood probably lies slumbering in every man, but it has more difficulty in some than in others in waking up. It needs the wilder passions to arouse it, the big fears, loves, and indignations."[32] The strenuous moral mood is the opposite of what James calls the "easy-going moral mood." James is sparing in his description of the easy-going moral mood, save for indicating that when we are in it, "the shrinking from present ill is our ruling consideration."[33] At the least, it is clear that the strenuous moral mood is animated by deliberate activity, whereas the easy-going moral mood is characterized more by passivity. Contrasting the opposed moral moods, James invokes martial metaphor, stating, "the strenuous type of character will on the battle-field of human history always outwear the easy-going type."[34] While it would be inaccurate to suggest that Mencius's picture of moral cultivation calls for passivity—it is a process requiring persistent and attentive action—Mencius's notion of moral cultivation is less obviously consistent with the strenuous moral mood as that of Xunzi.[35] While Mencius regards good morality as the natural course of things, when unimpeded by external forces, Xunzi would agree with James that "wilder passions" must arouse a conviction for and commitment to the moral life.[36] In this light, James's "moral equivalent of war" may be interpreted as a program intended to inspire the strenuous moral mood in youth, curbing incidents of violence and fostering the presence of peace.

CONCLUSION

In describing Xunzi's theory of human nature, Bryan W. Van Norden writes, "We must, Xunzi claimed, engage in the moral equivalent of war against our desires, and submerge ourselves in ritual (under the guidance of a good teacher), for a large part of our lives, before we will truly be fully moral."[37] With no explicit reference to James, it seems that the use of "the moral equivalent of war" here is coincidental, but as I have shown, it is by no means inappropriate. I have been arguing that there is a strong affinity between the thought of Xunzi and James on the subjects of human nature and morality. Keeping with the scholarly convention of contrasting Xunzi with Mencius, I have identified moments at which James's thought is not only reminiscent of that of Xunzi but apparently unlike that of Mencius. While I still maintain that James's thought is more akin to that of Xunzi, compartmentalizing James's thought is a slippery affair, and there is undoubtedly a Mencian aspect present in his ruminations on human nature. The vignette James shares about his train ride home from what he regards as an overly bucolic vacation in Chautauqua in "What Makes a Life Significant" (1899) is illustrative:

> . . . the sight of a workman doing something on the dizzy edge of a sky-scaling iron construction brought me to my senses suddenly. And now I perceived, by a flash of insight, that I had been steeping myself in pure ancestral blindness, and looking at life with the eyes of a remote spectator. Wishing for heroism and the spectacle of human nature on the rack, I had never noticed the great fields of heroism lying round about me, I had failed to see it present and alive. . . . Not in clanging fights and desperate marches only is heroism to be looked for, but on every railway bridge and fire-proof building that is going up to-day. On freight-trains, on the decks of vessels, in

cattle-yards and mines, on lumber-rafts, among the firemen and the policemen, the demand for courage is incessant; and the supply never fails. There, every day of the year somewhere, is human nature *in extremis* for you. And wherever a scythe, an axe, a pick, or a shovel is wielded, you have it sweating and aching and with its power of patient endurance racked to the utmost under the length of hours of the strain.[38]

That James describes the heroism of the ordinary laborer as "human nature *in extremis*" suggests an association with Mencius's thinking. Here James bears witness to the great potential of human nature, not as a latent capability or potency, but overtly displayed in situations of precariousness and peril. Thus, a decade prior to his formulation of his "moral equivalent of war," he observed a number of individuals who had already cultivated the "strenuous moral mood," bringing to full flower that which fell fallow in "unspeakable Chautauqua,"[39] a place where there was "no sweat, except possibly the gentle moisture on the brow of some lecturer, or on the sides of some player in the ball-field,"[40] and "no point of the compass visible from which danger might possibly appear."[41] Mencius and James are thus agreed that suitable environmental conditions must be in place for moral cultivation to transpire. There is, however, difference contained in the similarity. While Mencius regards the presence of individuals who have embodied virtues such as *ren* and *yi* as the nutrients necessary for moral cultivation, James suggests that the conditions requisite for moral cultivation are quite different. In order to become our best selves, we need to be immersed in a hostile environment, one that presses us to confront and grapple with obstacles of various types. Perhaps for James, the lover of paradox, it is fitting that the environment most nourishing of human nature and morality is replete with conflict.

5

Confucianism and Royce

Shame and Atonement

INTRODUCTION

The primary concern of moral philosophy is to clearly determine what counts as right or wrong action. Less attention is paid, however, to what counts as right action *once wrong action has been performed.* Much of the literature asks how to justly penalize the wrongdoer in the aftermath of the wrongdoing. In recent years, however, scholars have devoted more attention to the moral psychology of the wrongdoer and the obligations incumbent on him in the wake of his wrongdoing.[1] In this chapter, I take a similar approach to the subject of wrongdoing, by focusing on the phenomena of shame and atonement, placing the thought of Confucius and Mencius in dialogue with that of Josiah Royce. In so doing, I challenge Lee H. Yearley's claim that "virtues in Christianity, such as forgiveness and repentance, are not, for good or ill, prominent in Confucian accounts."[2] Considering the thought of Confucius and Mencius in light of that of Royce facilitates seeing how such virtues are indeed operative in their accounts.

Although Royce had an abiding interest in Asian philosophies, his attention seems to have been drawn more toward thought originating in India and Japan than that from China. Still, he seems to have cultivated at least a vague awareness of Chinese traditions, perhaps indirectly through his contact with other Asian traditions. Royce took a keen interest in Bushido, the ethical code of the Japanese samurai, with which he became acquainted from reading Inazo Nitobe's *Bushido: The Soul of Japan* (1900).³ Upon describing the Japanese samurai as an embodiment of important features of loyalty in *The Philosophy of Loyalty* (1908), Royce comments, "Chinese sages, as well as Buddhistic traditions, influenced his views of the cultivation of this interior self-possession and serenity of soul."⁴ Nitobe was undoubtedly Royce's source for this information. In the second chapter of *Bushido*, "The Sources of Bushido," Nitobe cites Buddhism, Shintoism, and Confucianism as the wellsprings of Bushido. For the latter source, Confucius and Mencius are, of course, integral. "As to strictly ethical doctrines," Nitobe states, "the teachings of Confucius were the most prolific source of Bushido."⁵ Moreover, "Mencius exercised an immense authority over Bushido."⁶ Germane to the focus of this chapter is Nitobe's remark: "Mencius had taught centuries before, in almost the identical phrase, what Carlyle has latterly expressed,—namely, that 'Shame is the soil of all Virtue, of good manners and good morals.'"⁷

Royce's most worked-out notions of shame and atonement come in the context of discussions of a theological bent. These swaths of text come in treatments of philosophical questions in which theological vocabulary is used either because the subject clearly calls for it (e.g., a discussion of the nature of God) or because it affords what Royce thinks to be a familiar and useful framework or application of ideas that are broader in scope (e.g., an application of his ethical theory to the case of Christian community). In discussing Royce's philosophy, I will draw on *The Conception of God* (1897), *The World and the Individual* (1901), *The Sources of Religious Insight* (1912), and *The Problem of Christianity* (1913), each of which is a prime example of Royce using theologically laden vocabulary to address a broad range of questions in metaphysics, ethics, and social philosophy.

When discussing "shame," it is helpful to distinguish between this concept and that of "guilt." Numerous studies in psychology, anthropology, philosophy, and other fields have distinguished between these terms differently. For my purposes, the following generally accepted distinction will suffice. Guilt is typically understood as a feeling of responsibility for a wrongdoing one has performed. According to an early study by Wolfram Eberhard, feelings of guilt in traditional China were associated with "violations or transgressions in the field of social relations—that is, social role behavior."[8] Shame is typically understood as a negative feeling caused by awareness of something dishonorable done by oneself or another. As Eberhard details, the most common Chinese term for "shame" (*chi* 耻) "is written with the determinant 'ear' and the word for 'heart' and is explained by lexicographers as a feeling which causes one's ears to become red."[9] To further clarify the distinction, imagine that you are borrowing a book from a friend, and you assure your friend that you will return the book in one week, knowing that you will not return it for at least a month. Sooner or later, it is likely that you will experience guilt, aware that you are responsible for creating the expectation that the book would be returned on time and the disappointment when it is not. You might then experience shame, a feeling aroused by recognizing the kind of person that you have allowed yourself to become—someone who is dishonest and who abuses the trust of a friend. Moreover, it is possible that someone associated with you knows what you have done and feels shame because of your action. For example, your mother might feel ashamed by your actions. But it is impossible for her to feel guilt (or at least her doing so would be misdirected), as she is not responsible for the wrongdoing.

When I use "atonement," I follow the definition recorded in the *Oxford English Dictionary*: "The action of setting at one or condition of being set at one, after discord or strife."[10] This definition suggests that atonement involves some sort of correction or repair in the wake of incorrect or injurious action. This definition does *not* suggest that atonement is an exclusively theological concept. While atonement may take the form of a sinner making amends with God, it may also be situated in a secular context, such as human beings making amends for wrongdoings done to one another. To continue with the example that I used to distinguish between guilt and shame, you may atone for the wrongdoing of the false promise with respect to returning your friend's book punctually by apologizing, returning the book, and vowing to your friend that your dishonesty and disrespect will cease. Given this understanding of "atonement," it is plausible that early Confucian philosophers address atonement, even if a neat correlate to the term is not operative in their vocabulary. Although Royce's discussion of atonement occurs within a broader discussion of Christianity, his theory of atonement is explicitly intended for all individuals and communities regardless of religious affiliation.[11]

I will begin by considering the concept of "shame" in Royce's thought. Because he *does not* appear to draw a rigid distinction between shame and guilt, I will consider some of his writing focused on the latter, as well. I will discuss how shame and guilt are connected to immorality, with attention to Royce's notion of sin. I will ask whether, for Royce, shame is a good thing or bad thing. I will then discuss shame in the context of early Confucianism. As with my discussion of Royce, I will inquire as to what sorts of wrongdoing can be rightly understood as causing shame. I will also raise the question of the benefits and harms of shame. Next, I will give sketches of some theories of atonement. Doing this will set the stage for discussing the role of atonement in the philosophy of Royce. Finally, building from this foundation, I will propose a theory of atonement present in early Confucian thought.

SHAME IN THE THOUGHT OF ROYCE

Recall the distinction drawn earlier between guilt and shame: Guilt is typically understood as a feeling of responsibility for a wrongdoing one has performed. Shame is typically understood as a negative feeling caused by awareness of something dishonorable done by oneself or another. Mentions of shame in Royce's writing are scant, whereas mentions of guilt are more plentiful. The paucity of mentions of shame is an obstacle to this comparative analysis, for Royce seems not to draw a neat distinction between shame and guilt. For this reason, I will briefly examine one case of Royce discussing shame and one case of his discussing guilt. I will then link his comments on shame and guilt with his conception of wrongdoing.

Insufficient credit is given to Royce's psychological thought, which includes a remarkably robust moral psychology.[12] Sometimes Royce forays into this conceptual territory in unexpected places, such as in the supplementary essay to *The Conception of God*. Here, Royce describes moral development in terms of increasing the data of our self-consciousness by contrasting ourselves with others:

> More complex grows the contrast of the ego and non-ego when my attention is not merely attracted to the states of my neighbour's mind as indicated to me in one region of my mental life, and as thus directly contrasted with mine, but is also attracted to the fact that my neighbour is aware of me, has his opinion of me, and is concerned in me very much as I am concerned in him. For now I learn to contrast my neighbour's view of me, not only with my states as they already exist in me, but also with the view of myself that hereupon, by virtue of my natural vanity, modesty, obstinacy, or plasticity, gets aroused in me as my response to his conceived opinion of me. My neighbour approves me. And now I both note and value myself more. My neighbour dislikes my looks, my actions, my voice, the selfishness of my behaviour. I come also to take note of this view of myself. It arouses a response of resentment, of contempt, of shame, of obstinacy, of desire to reform, or of wish that I were another.[13]

The contrast of the ego and non-ego, or self and non-self, is brought into sharp relief in emotional states such as shame.[14] The experience of shame involves the acute awareness of any of a number of contrasts. I may come to recognize the difference between others and myself, the disparity between myself and what others think of me, the gap between my ideal self and my real self. Shame, then, involves a contestation between who I am and who I ought to be.

Royce's discussion of guilt in *The Sources of Religious Insight* reveals that he does not draw a sharp distinction between this concept and that of shame. Seeming to echo his description of shame from *The Conception of God*, Royce writes, "Now the sense of guilt, if deep and pervasive and passionate, involves at least a dim recognition that there is some central aim of life and that one has come hopelessly short of that aim."[15] In other words (and to repeat what Royce says in his description of shame), when I feel guilt, I am conscious of a gap between who I am and who I ought to be. In this awareness, I may experience a number of thoughts and emotions. According to Royce, "We all know how the sense of guilt may take the form of a feeling of overwhelming loneliness."[16] The feeling of loneliness may not be desirable, but guilt can produce even deeper psychological effects. As he puts it, "the true sense of guilt in its greater manifestation involves a confession that the whole self is somehow tainted, the whole life, for the time being, wrecked."[17] Note that Royce's use of "guilt" goes beyond that of typical contemporary parlance. This guilt is not simply acknowledgment of responsibility for wrongdoing. It is a profound feeling of dishonor, provoked by the sort of action I have performed and/or the sort of person I have become. Whatever the "central aim of life" it is that I have fallen short of, I am left feeling that my being is tainted, even perhaps that my life is a wreck.

It is evident that Royce conceives of shame and guilt primarily as emotions felt when contrasting oneself with another or with an ideal, recognizing that one has failed in some regard. Acts of wrongdoing are not the only instigators of shame and guilt, but it seems that for Royce, they are primary. One of Royce's most explicit treatments of the machinations of wrongdoing occurs in his discussion of sin in *The World and the Individual*, delivered as the Gifford Lectures at the University of Aberdeen. In this text, Royce draws a parallel between sin and the limits of human consciousness: "every least shifting of our conscious momentary attention is one of these small steps whereby we continually undertake to make good the original sin, as it were, with which our form of consciousness is beset."[18] The world is one of infinite detail, but the nature of our being is such that we are only able to pay close attention to a small portion of it at once; the remainder exists merely as a vague background. Despite our finite consciousness, we consciously wish to know the world better than we do. Royce dubs the conflict between our perpetually having this desire and our fundamental incapability of satisfying it a "tragedy of satisfaction through the establishment and the overcoming of endless dissatisfaction."[19] This situation is tragic, for as soon as we are able to direct our conscious awareness to some field with which it has not yet been acquainted, we find ourselves wanting to widen its scope again; our satisfactions carry with them new dissatisfactions to be overcome. This is the situation of beings characterized by finitude. "*Our finitude,*" explains Royce, "*means then, an actual inattention,—a lack of successful interest, at this conscious instant, in more than a very few of the details of the universe.*"[20] Although Royce does not immediately comment as to whether sin simply amounts to this inattention to particular details of the universe, he revisits the subject several lectures later:

> To sin is *consciously to choose to forget*, through a narrowing of the field of attention, an Ought that one already recognizes. For while I cannot avoid acting in accordance with the Ought so long as I clearly know it, I can, through voluntary *inattention*, freely choose to forget it. . . . all sin is a free choosing of the *sort* of narrowness which, in our second lecture, we found to be, in one aspect, the natural fate of the human being.[21]

In being deliberately inattentive to a moral obligation, the sinner "forgets God as God, forgets the Ought as the Ought, and acts with a viciously acquired naiveté."[22]

It bears repeating that while Royce uses theologically laden terms in this discussion, his intention is to discuss the human situation in general.[23] His discussion of the sinner can be secularized to a discussion of the wrongdoer or the moral agent who acts immorally. In fact, Royce does not exclusively use "sinner" in this context, but he frequently uses "moral agent" and "individual" to refer to the subject. The phenomenon of knowing what one ought to do and casting a blind eye to that obligation is one familiar to all humans, irrespective of religious belief or affiliation.[24] It is also one that is liable to cause shame. Indeed, this seems to be exactly the sort of experience that Royce has in mind when referring to the profound disappointment experienced when one comes up short with respect to a central aim of life. "I may regret a blunder," Royce states, but "a blunder is a special affair involving the missing of some particular aim."[25] Guilt runs deeper than regret. It is occasioned not by missing an aim, but by *choosing* to miss an aim. Given this distinction, Royce's description of a guilt-ridden person evaluating his life as a wreck is dramatic, but by no means unrealistic.

SHAME IN THE THOUGHT OF CONFUCIUS AND MENCIUS

There is no more direct statement of the importance of shame in Confucian philosophy than that from Mencius at *Mencius* 7A6: "A person must not be without shame. Shamelessness is the shame of being without shame." This unequivocal affirmation of the significance of shame raises the question of what "shame" amounts to for Mencius and other early Confucians. According to Jane Geaney, "Something like a contact-driven, boundary-blurring model of shame is what emerges clearly" in an analysis of the references to shame in the classical Confucian texts.[26] Indeed, occurrences of the notion of shame (*chi* 耻) are often associated with impropriety with respect to boundaries related to identity or social status. In the *Analects* and the *Mencius* (and the *Xunzi*), people are portrayed as feeling shame (or it is remarked that they ought to feel shame) in response to actions that push or blur boundaries that ought to be observed. Bongrae Seok distinguishes between two contrasting senses of *chi* in Confucian philosophy: external *chi* and internal *chi*, calling external *chi* "a shameful experience caused by one's bad or inferior exterior (i.e., appearance, cloth[ing], behavior, etc.), typically in front of or in comparison with others" and internal *chi* "an inner sense of morality, such as the sense of modesty, honor, or appropriateness."[27] To illustrate this distinction, I want to consider a number of excerpts from the *Analects* and *Mencius*. These exemplify external *chi*:

> The Master said, "A scholar-official who has set his heart upon the *dao*, but who is still ashamed of having shabby clothing or meager rations, is not worth engaging in discussion." (*Analects* 4.9)[28]

> To be the servant of others yet ashamed of his service is like the maker of bows who is ashamed of making bows or the maker of arrows who is ashamed of making arrows. If one is ashamed of this, there is nothing better than to be *ren*. One who would be *ren* is like the archer. The archer corrects his

position and then shoots. If he shoots and misses he does not blame those who are more adept than he; rather, he turns within and seeks within himself. (*Mencius* 2A7)

Meanwhile, these excerpts exemplify internal *chi*:

The Master said, "People in ancient times were not eager to speak, because they would be ashamed if their actions did not measure up to their words." (*Analects* 4.22)[29]

To occupy a humble position and speak of lofty matters is a crime. To stand in the ruler's court and not have the *dao* carried into practice is shameful. (*Mencius* 5B5)

Lines between external and internal shame may not always be neatly drawn. It is conceivable that external shame and internal shame could be experienced simultaneously. In *Mencius* 2A7, for instance, one may feel external shame at the behavior of one's ruler, and internal shame at having not adequately searched within oneself to determine how to be a more effective positive influence.

However we parse *chi* in these passages, it is clear enough that *having a sense of shame* is a good thing, as it indicates sensitivity to values. On the other hand, *being ashamed* is of ambiguous moral value. It is bad if one is ashamed for the wrong reason (e.g., being ashamed of one's clothing[30] and meager rations as in *Analects* 4.9, or being ashamed of serving one's ruler as in *Mencius* 2A7).[31] It is good, however, if caused by the right thing—although the "right thing" in this context is typically something less than admirable (e.g., feeling shame if one's actions fail to measure up to one's words as in *Analects* 4.22, or holding an official position and failing to make a positive moral impact as in *Mencius* 5B5). It seems that one who has a sense of shame (what we might call good *chi*) is less likely to behave in a way that causes shame in oneself or in others (what we might call bad *chi*).

It is instructive to see shame in the Confucian context in terms of disharmony. Nathaniel F. Barrett argues that as experiences of disharmony, experiences of shame "provide intimations of values that are marginalized and thereby diminished in our experience, or . . . that indicate harmonies in which we cannot participate effectively."³² What sorts of experiences warrant shame is at least in part a product of cultural norms. In the Confucian context, the patterns of ritual (*li* 禮) serve as a guide as to what sort of harmonies one should seek:

> Master You said, "When it comes to the practice of *li*, it is harmonious ease that is to be valued. It is precisely such harmony that makes the *dao* of the Former Kings so beautiful. If you merely stick rigidly to ritual in all matters, great and small, there will remain that which you cannot accomplish. Yet if you know enough to value harmonious ease but try to attain it without being regulated by *li*, this will not work either." (*Analects* 1.12)

Barrett is correct to see this passage as "an indication of a circular relationship between *li* and harmony."³³ *Li* show us what sort of harmonies we should seek, and what is more, *li* are practiced for the sake of harmony.³⁴ Having a sense of shame conduces toward harmony, encouraging behavior recognized by our community as good and discouraging behavior recognized by our community as bad. When we act in ways disruptive of harmony, we might feel shame; disrupting harmony and not experiencing attendant shame is indicative of dysfunction in a significant part of our morality. Shame is thus important for both the individual and the community. It is an experience that helps to fortify individual character (or is indicative of fortified character), while at the same time it is a property that binds communities.

In early Confucian texts, shame is often induced by an incongruity between one's words and one's actions, or between one's reputation and one's true character. The *Analects* and *Mencius* are replete with examples of such cases, as is evident from passages already considered. I want to examine one additional passage from the *Analects* and two additional passages from the *Mencius*, explicating them through the vocabulary for shame that has been developed to this point, via both early Confucian thought and Royce's thought:

The Master said, "Clever words, an ingratiating countenance, and perfunctory gestures of respect are all things that Zuoqiu Ming considered shameful, and I, too, consider them shameful. Concealing one's resentment and feigning friendship toward another is something Zuoqiu considered shameful, and I, too, consider it shameful." (*Analects* 5.25)

Mencius said, "Words that do not correspond to reality are unfortunate, and what is really most unfortunate is to obscure the reputation of a person of ability." (*Mencius* 4B17)

Xuzi said, "Confucius often praised water, saying, 'Ah, Water! Water!' What was it that he found in water?"
Mencius said, "A spring of water gushing forth rests neither day nor night. It fills the hollows and then moves on to reach the four seas. What has a source is like this, and this is what he found worthy of praise. If there is no source, then in the seventh and eighth months, when the rain falls copiously, the channels in the fields are all filled, yet one may expect that they will soon be dried up again. Therefore, the *junzi* is ashamed to have a reputation that exceeds actuality." (*Mencius* 4B18)

In *Analects* 5.25, Confucius identifies as shameful the behavior of deliberately placing a boundary between one's true character and one's public image, leading to the blurring of that boundary in the eyes of those who do not know one's true character. Smooth talk,[35] appearance, and pretense of respect are just some of the ways this duplicity is promulgated.[36] In *Mencius* 4B17, Mencius registers a similar criticism of those who are duplicitous in obscuring the reputation of people deserving of a good reputation. Although *chi* does not appear in this passage, the notion is more than likely implicit in "most unfortunate." Concealing resentment and feigning friendship (in *Analects* 5.25) are varieties of dishonesty and, as such, are worthy of inducing shame. If one connives in any of these ways, one ought to feel shame (i.e., internal shame). As Mencius says in *Mencius* 4B18, the *junzi* feels shame if his reputation exceeds actuality. It is not necessarily the case that the *junzi* has self-aggrandized such that his reputation exceeds actuality, but the misalignment between his renown and his true character is something that he should attend to, particularly if he is known to be virtuous when he is not.

In all of these cases, there is a disharmony between the agent and *li*, and recurrent throughout these passages is the notion that a failure to follow *li* should bring about in the agent a feeling of shame. For Royce, each of these instances of mendacity could be understood as sin, insofar as each is a deliberate inattention to an *Ought*.[37] As we saw in chapter 4, Mencius believes that our natural tendency is toward *ren*, *yi*, *li*, and *zhi*: "We definitely possess them. It is just that we do not think about it, that is all. Therefore it is said, 'Seek and you will get it; let go and you will lose it'" (*Mencius* 6A6). Perhaps these acts of wrongdoing may be understood as "letting go" (i.e., intentionally not thinking about one's basic goodness) in order to rationalize acting badly. In *Analects* 5.25, the agent purposefully narrows his consciousness in order to focus on the impression that he wishes to make on the other, ignoring his awareness that it is better, morally, to be honest. In *Mencius* 4B17, the agent who has narrowed his consciousness of the character of the person of ability, speaking ill of the person to damage his repute, also consciously ignores a wealth of facts (about the person of ability, about the importance of truth in speech) that he knows to be true. In *Mencius* 4B18, the *junzi* would be ashamed to narrow his consciousness in such a way as to convince himself that he measures up to his reputation when he knows that he really does not.

Whether any of these agents would entertain the degree of self-critical evaluative thoughts that Royce imagines is an open question. We can presume, however, that Confucius and Mencius prefer that agents of such description have a robust enough sense of shame to recognize these faults as faults and recalibrate their efforts to follow the *dao*. If this presumption is justified—and there is ample textual evidence to suggest that it is—then we have some indication of the presence of a notion of atonement in early Confucian thought. Before delving into that matter, it will be instructive to first outline the most common conceptions of atonement. Given his explicit and sustained discussion of this concept, I will then examine Royce's thought on atonement. I will follow this discussion by taking up atonement in the thought of Confucius.

THEORIES OF ATONEMENT

Scholars have advocated several notions of atonement, and it will be helpful to distinguish among some of the most prevalent conceptions, even if only in broad strokes.[38] Retributive theories of atonement hold that wrongdoers deserve to suffer some sort of loss or penalty as a just response to their wrongdoing. Because wronging another person involves incurring a moral debt, atoning for wrongdoing involves repaying the debt. Restitutive theories of atonement hold that wrongdoers should present their victims with a form of compensation that is proportional to the wrongdoing. Pure restitution theory does not include any special interest in the suffering of wrongdoers as such, whereas punitive restitution theory maintains that the suffering of wrongdoers is an important and sometimes uniquely appropriate means of paying restitution to the victim of wrongdoing.[39] Reformative theories of atonement hold that atonement requires transformation—of the character of the wrongdoer and the wrongdoer's commitments, on one hand, and of the meaning of past events and expectations of future events, on the other. Reconciliatory theories of atonement hold that the wrongdoer should act so as to restore a relationship or relationships in some way damaged by his wrongdoing, including his own relationships (e.g., with his community, with himself), and those of his victim (e.g., the victim's relationship with himself and his community), sometimes including the prior relationship between the wrongdoer and the victim. In the next two sections, it will be useful to remember these terms and distinctions.

ATONEMENT IN THE THOUGHT OF ROYCE

In *The Problem of Christianity*, Royce offers a theory of atonement centering on the figure of the traitor. As described by Royce, the betrayal the traitor performs is against an ideal that he has loved with "all his heart and his soul and his mind and his strength."[40] Before the act of treason, he had embraced the ideal with the utmost loyalty. In his treason, however, he has performed "a wilful closing of his eyes to the light,"[41] having been "deliberately false to his cause"[42] in at least one voluntary act of his life. These two conditions—possession and cherishing of an ideal, and voluntary falseness to this ideal—comprise the two conditions constituting treason. Adopting Royce's language from *The World and the Individual*, the traitor is one who has sinned, for he has been deliberately inattentive to an Ought, the Ought expressed in the ideal that he has cherished. This situation induces in the traitor a deep sense of shame: "The more precious the light that has seemed to come to me, the deeper is the disgrace to which, in my own eyes, I can condemn myself, if I voluntarily become false to this light."[43]

Royce frequently refers to the situation of the traitor as tragic. The situation of the traitor is tragic in the sense that any human being is a victim of the tragic. As a finite being, he is destined to at some time be deliberately inattentive to a moral obligation (i.e., to commit wrongdoing, to sin). In this way, he has done what he cannot help but do; he has expressed the very nature of his being, finitude, through what is considered an immoral act. As depicted by Royce, the case of the traitor is especially tragic, in that his immoral act is not just a betrayal of an ideal but also a betrayal of a community of which he is a member. As Royce puts it, "he destroyed by his deed the community in whose brotherhood, in whose life, in whose spirit, he had found his guide and his ideal."[44] More than this, nothing that the traitor may do will ever undo his treason. "In that sense," explains Royce, ". . . no good deeds of the traitor's future will ever *so* atone for his one act of treason."[45]

While the traitor and community must forever reside in "the hell of the irrevocable,"[46] Royce urges, "Great calamities are great opportunities."[47] Royce thinks it conceivable that the traitor might become reconciled to himself, to his deed, and to the meaning of his deed in his moral world, even if "it will be at best but an imperfect and tragic reconciliation."[48] Royce distinguishes between forgiveness and reconciliation, understanding the former as "an affectionate remission of penalty."[49] Reconciliation entails forgiveness, but it is more than this; it is "a restoring of the love of the community, or of its members, towards the one who has now sinned, but repented."⁵⁰ Royce's theory of atonement is clearly aimed at reconciliation. But how is this reconciliation to be accomplished? Royce thinks it crucial that the act of treason concerns not just the traitor but the community of which he is a member. One must therefore additionally ask whether the *community* can reconcile itself to the deeds of the traitor.

Just as in the case of the traitor, the reconciliation that might be achieved by the community will never be complete; the life of the community "can never be restored to its former purity of unscarred love."⁵¹ Even if the community exacts a penalty against the traitor, the effects of such action are limited: "Penalty, even if called for, annuls nothing of all that has been done. Repentance does not turn backward the flow of time."⁵² Thus, the process of redemption is doubly tragic. While the traitor must forever reside in "the hell of the irrevocable," knowing that it will always be the case that he did the deed in question, the community must reside there too, knowing that it will always be the case that its unity was shattered by the traitorous act.⁵³ Just as the community must face that it has irrevocably lost its "unscarred love," the traitor is left to acknowledge soberly, "That fact, that event, that deed, is irrevocable. The fact that I am the one who then did thus and so, not ignorantly, but knowingly,—that fact will outlast the ages. That fact is as endless as time."⁵⁴

For Royce, however, the calamity of treason is, in fact, a great opportunity. Treason acts as the precondition for the opportunity of the fortification of the individual and the community issuing from acts of atonement. Reconciliation is not to be *found* but to be *created*, and "this creative work shall include a deed, or various deeds, for which only just this treason furnishes the opportunity."⁵⁵ Thus, "*The world, as transformed by this creative deed, is better than it would have been had all else remained the same, but had that deed of treason not been done at all.*"⁵⁶ Consequently, while Royce's theory of atonement should be seen as a reconciliatory theory of atonement, it should also be seen as a reformative theory of atonement. Atonement transforms the meaning of a past event and the expectation of future events. On the part of the traitor, the creative act "breaks open, as it were, the tomb of the dead and treacherous past, and comes forth as the life and the expression of the creative and reconciling will."[57] On the part of the community, the creative act "transforms the meaning of that very past which it cannot undo" via a "transfiguration of the very loss into a gain that, without this very loss, could never have been won."[58]

Although penalty and compensation might still figure in the behavior of the atoning agent, it is evident that Royce's theory of atonement calls for reconciliation and reformation. Royce acknowledges the singular and communal components of sin and addresses each by providing both a way in which the individual guilty of transgression can achieve reconciliation with himself, the community of which he is a member can achieve reconciliation with itself, and the two can achieve reconciliation with each other. Admittedly, these reconciliations are necessarily tragic. While atonement can be carried out with success, the success of this process is hopelessly limited: "Repentance does not turn backwards the flow of time."[59] Nonetheless, it is precisely because the flow of time continues forward that atonement is necessary.[60]

ATONEMENT IN THE THOUGHT OF CONFUCIUS

I want to emphasize once more that Royce's notions of sin and atonement need not be confined to the theological frameworks through which Royce deploys them. Taking these concepts at their essential meanings for Royce, they can be stripped of their Christian clothing and found to be more or less congruent with concepts from Confucian philosophy. I have already demonstrated this in the case of the compatibility between Royce's notion of sin and varieties of *chi* that abound in the early Confucian texts.[61] I propose that the same is true of Royce's notion of atonement. Taken simply as a form of reconciliation between a moral agent who has betrayed an ideal and, in the process, betrayed a community, a cogent case can be made for the presence of a theory of atonement in early Confucian thought. I find the most compelling case in the thought of Confucius, so I will for the very most part limit my textual focus to the *Analects*.[62]

We have seen in previous chapters some passages from the *Analects* that are relevant to the present discussion. For example, in *Analects* the neighborhood of *ren* is fine. If one does not choose to dwell among those who are *ren*, how will one obtain wisdom?"

These are not merely prescriptive pronouncements, however, for Confucius is portrayed in the *Analects* as having himself lived up to these ideals:

> The Master said, "That I fail to cultivate virtue, that I fail to inquire more deeply into that which I have learned, that upon hearing what is right I remain unable to move myself to do it, and that I prove unable to reform when I have done something wrong—such potential failings are a source of constant worry to me." (*Analects* 7.3)

That the inability to reform when he has done something wrong is a source of *constant* worry to Confucius ought not to go unnoticed.[64] In light of this self-assessment, we ought not to be surprised when Confucius reveals in *Analects* 7.22, "I focus on those who are good and seek to emulate them, and focus on those who are bad in order to be reminded of what needs to be changed in myself." We can infer that Confucius acknowledges the *possibility* of his performing transgressions, though as a number of episodes in the *Analects* illustrate, Confucius *does* occasionally commit transgressions, albeit relatively minor ones.[65] There is no clear evidence, however, that he fails to reform upon having done so.[66]

His own case aside, Confucius expresses exasperation at having not met anyone who lives up to this standard: "The Master said, 'I should just give up! I have yet to meet someone who is able to perceive his own faults and then take himself to task inwardly'" (*Analects* 5.27). Perhaps inconsistent on this point,[67] Confucius does identify one person who is able to do these things—his best disciple, Yan Hui. Unfortunately, Yan Hui's case is indeed exceptional, and ephemeral:

> Duke Ai asked, "Who among your disciples might be said to love learning?"
>
> Confucius answered, "There was one named Yan Hui who loved learning. He never misdirected his anger and never made the same mistake twice. Unfortunately, his allotted lifespan

was short, and he has passed away. Now that he is gone, there are none who really love learning—at least, I have yet to hear of one." (*Analects* 6.3)

We can conclude that Confucius regards as rare the recognition of one's own wrongdoing and the concomitant effort to improve oneself in light of such recognition.

This dual recognition and reformation is as important as it is rare:

> The Master said, "When a man is rebuked with exemplary words after having made a mistake, he cannot help but agree with them. However, what is important is that he change himself in order to *accord* with them. When a man is praised with words of respect, he cannot help but be pleased with them. However, what is important is that he actually *live up* to them. A person who finds respectful words pleasing but does not live up to them, or agrees with others' reproaches and yet does not change—there is nothing I can do with one such as this." (*Analects* 9.24, emphasis in original)

It is clear enough that Confucius calls for rectification of one's behavior in light of one's wrongdoing, consistently underscoring the importance of doing so and the apparent infrequency with which he observes it being done. Perhaps because he so often addresses disciples who are wont to occasional transgressions, this is the emphasis most clearly struck in his remarks on this subject.

Still, there is at least one occasion on which Confucius addresses the other side of the coin: "The Master said, 'Bo Yi and Shu Qi did not harbor grudges. For this reason, they aroused little resentment'" (*Analects* 5.23). Here, Confucius offers Bo Yi and Shu Qi as admirable examples, for their willingness to forgive. One could suggest that Confucius's admiration of the pair lies in their ability to avoid arousing resentment—not in any positive value associated with not harboring grudges. But if their avoidance of arousing resentment stems from an artificial façade, Confucius would likely not condone their behavior, let alone commend it. Bo Yi is cast in a favorable light in several passages in the *Mencius*, with Mencius even referring to him as "the sage who was pure" (*Mencius* 5B1).[68] Slingerland quotes Zhu Xi as saying that Bo Yi's "dislike of a person ceased immediately once that person was able to change his fault."[69] On this description, we can infer that Confucius admires both Bo Yi's (and Shu Qi's) ability to recognize bad behavior when they see it and their ability to appreciate efforts to reform such that the moral status of the agent is not crystallized by his transgressions.

We have seen that Confucius thinks that what is important is that a person who makes a mistake *change himself* in order to accord with exemplary words.[70] At the least, Confucian atonement involves a revision of one's character, and thus of one's habits of action. Although textual evidence is less clear on this point, we have also seen that Confucius thinks forgiveness of those who have done so is commendable. If Confucius teaches by example, and highlights the example of individuals whose habit was to respond to a wrongdoer's reform by shedding grudges, then such behavior is probably recommended and not merely supererogatory. In any case, because Confucian atonement involves correction of one's character, it is not simply a matter of incurring punishment or proffering some sort of repayment.

In fact, we have already seen clear indication that Confucius would not advocate retributive thinking about atonement.[71] Recall *Analects* 2.3:

> The Master said: "If you try to guide the common people with coercive regulations and keep them in line with punishments, the common people will become evasive and will have no sense of shame. If, however, you guide them with virtue, and keep them in line by means of ritual, the people will have a sense of shame and will rectify themselves."

Add to this passage *Analects* 12.19:

> Ji Kangzi asked Confucius about governing, saying, "If I were to execute those who lacked the *dao* in order to advance those who possessed the *dao*, how would that be?"

> Confucius responded, "In your governing, Sir, what need is there for executions? If you desire goodness, then the common people will be good. The virtue of a *junzi* is like the wind, and the virtue of a *xiaoren* is like the grass—when the wind moves over the grass, the grass is sure to bend."

Because Confucius thinks that rulers ought not to rely upon punitive measures to inculcate order in the community, it is reasonable to assume that Confucius would not stray from this position when it comes to restoring order when it has been disrupted by an act of wrongdoing. This is not to suggest that Confucius is altogether opposed to punishments for wrongdoing, but it is to suggest that Confucius does not regard punishments as sufficient for dealing with the presence of wrongdoing. Effective governing will instill in the people a sense of shame, such that they will normally not be compelled to commit acts of wrongdoing, and when they are, they will recognize the harm done by their transgression and willingly work to make amends.

It does not seem that Confucius would advocate restitutive thinking about atonement, either. At least, it seems that he would find restitutive theories of atonement only partially effective. Consider *Analects* 2.7: "Ziyou asked about filial conduct. The Master replied: 'Those today who are filial are considered so because they are able to provide for their parents. But even dogs and horses are given that much care. If you do not respect your parents, what is the difference?'" Here, Confucius complains that the notion of "filiality" has been diluted; sons and daughters providing basic necessities for their parents are dubbed "filial" when filiality really involves more than just this. To truly be filial, one must both act filially and *feel* filially. Interlacing the themes of atonement and filiality for a moment, imagine having broken a valuable item owned by your mother. It is an item that she has owned for several years, and it is emblematic of several cherished memories. Your filial obligation would surely be to address the wrongdoing and atone for the damage done in some way. Imagine not expressing any regret at having broken the item, nor of the distress that you caused her at having done so. Instead, you simply write her a check for the monetary value of the item. To do so would, in a sense, make amends for the loss. It would not, however, do so in a way that Confucius would find particularly meaningful, for it would not be accompanied by sincerity and respect. For Confucius, then, the atoning agent must be of a particular frame of mind or quality of character. In this example, the atoning agent would need to be characterized by *xiao*, though we may also speak more generally of *ren*, *de*, or *shu* 恕 (empathy, reciprocity).[72]

While Confucius does not seem to advocate retributive nor restitutive theories of atonement, it is fairly evident that he advocates some kind of reformative theory of atonement. I have considered several passages in which Confucius states clearly the importance of wrongdoers' reforming their character in light of their wrongdoing. It is not enough to recognize that one has made a mistake or deviated from the *dao*; it is necessary to redouble one's efforts to avoid doing so again. Only then can the transgression be regarded as a momentary misalignment in one's journey along the *dao*. To echo Royce, the calamity that is the wrongdoing of the past can be the opportunity to transform one's character and conduct in the future. A misstep in one's journey along the *dao* may become the impetus for charting that path in a more earnest and effective fashion than would have been possible if not for the misstep having occurred.

At this point, I think it is clear that Confucius advocates a reformative theory of atonement. What is less clear is whether Confucius also endorses a reconciliatory theory of atonement. Recall that reconciliation theories of atonement involve the wrongdoer's restoring a relationship(s) in some way damaged by his wrongdoing. One is pressed to find Confucius explicitly joining remarks about the importance of recognizing one's wrongdoing and the need to reform with remarks concerning the restoration of *relationships* in some way damaged by the wrongdoing. In my example inspired by *Analects* 2.7, we could imagine making up for having broken the object by not only writing a check for its monetary value but also apologizing sincerely and wanting for the distress caused by the broken item to be alleviated. Still, this need not include mending the relationship between mother and child, if this relationship has been shattered along with the object in question. Confucius would likely not be satisfied if the atoning agent made no effort to reconcile the filial relationship that had previously been shared.

Earlier, I suggested that comment about the importance of forgiveness could be drawn from the praise Confucius gives to Bo Yi and Shu Qi in *Analects* 5.23. Another passage in which Confucius praises a figure of semi-legendary status can be read as his conveying a teaching relevant to the present discussion. In *Analects* 11.5, Confucius is recorded as saying, "How filial is Min Ziqian! No one can gainsay the praise lavished upon him by both parents and brothers." The story of Min Ziqian would have been familiar to Confucius's disciples. I quote Slingerland's retelling of the story at length:

> Min Ziqian apparently lost his mother early in life, whereupon his father remarried and had two more sons with his new wife. The new wife hated Min Ziqian and treated him poorly, favoring her own two sons. One cold winter day, Ziqian was out driving for his father when the reins of the carriage fell from his hands; on examination, the father discovered that Ziqian's hands had frozen because he was wearing only thin, unlined gloves. Returning home and inspecting the hands of his new wife and her two sons, he discovered that they were clad in warm, padded gloves, and in his anger he wished to dismiss her and disown her children. Ziqian then interceded, saying, "While she is here, one son must go cold, but were she to be dismissed, three sons would be out in the cold"—i.e., without the stepmother, both Ziqian *and* his two stepbrothers would be bereft of a mother's love. The father relented, and according to some versions the stepmother, shamed by Ziqian's selflessness, reformed herself and became an exemplary parent.[73]

Confucius praises Min Ziqian for his unwavering filiality, which extended to his stepmother despite her malicious and harmful treatment of him. His filiality certainly is exceptional. One might regard it as *irrational*, given the victimization he suffered at her hands. The denouement mitigates such a judgment, showing that Min Ziqian's allowing his stepmother the opportunity to atone for her actions inspires her doing so. Subsequently, the various bonds across the family are strengthened. While Confucius's praise is directed at Min

Ziqian, it is not difficult to imagine his conferring praise to Min Ziqian's stepmother for undergoing a transformation of character, and to Min Ziqian's father for resisting the impulse to sever ties with his wife, heeding the remonstration of his son, and sustaining the cohesion of the family unit.

It is also not difficult to locate in this episode the various elements of Royce's treatments of shame and atonement. What occurs between the stepmother (as sinner/traitor) and the rest of the family (as the shattered community) maps neatly onto Royce's reconciliatory theory of atonement. As the story goes, the family is more strongly united than they had been before the stepmother's misdeed. The reconciliatory efforts made possible only by her transgression give rise to a family bond more marked by filiality than it would have been had the transgression not occurred in the first place.[74]

Consider also *Analects* 13.18, in which the Duke of She tells Confucius of "Upright Gong," a man who informed the authorities when his father stole a sheep. Confucius replies that where he is from, uprightness is different from this: "fathers cover up for their sons, and sons cover up for their fathers. 'Uprightness' is to be found in this." I would like to suggest the possibility of compatibility between Confucius's reply and Royce's reconciliatory theory of atonement.

Let us presume that this theft occurred because the father was in dire straits, desperate for food or whatever other resources the sheep will provide. The matter of who is to blame for the act of theft is open to several diagnoses. The father certainly should not allow himself to fall below decent moral standards. At the same time, if the theft arises from felt need, it may be that the son has not properly provided for his father. An interjection from Royce would be appropriate: "But we have in general no right to say with assurance, when we speak of our individual neighbors, that we know who the traitors are. For we are no searchers of hearts."[75] In any case, it is Confucius's view that upon finding that his father stole a sheep, the son should not have reported him to the authorities. If he did fail in his duties as a son, perhaps the next thing to do is to reform his behavior. One way of doing so would be to turn himself in,[76] accepting responsibility for having stolen the sheep. In this case, the son owns up to *his* wrongdoing and acts so as to reconcile his relationship with his father. In response, perhaps the father might think it his filial duty to admit to the authorities that it was he who stole the sheep, not his son. After all, he has transgressed against his son, too, by not serving as a moral role model and by allowing for his son to incur the shameful status as the son of the man who stole a sheep. It is not clear how such a turn of events would have gone over with the authorities,[77] but courses of action other than reporting his father to the authorities would have done more in the way of atonement. On this reading, reflecting a hybrid of Confucian and Roycean ideas, when a father covers for his son and a son covers for his father, each assumes his filial duty, reconciling each to the other. They do so presumably as an unusual and emphatic response to tragic events that have arisen from a lapse in the maintenance of such duties. Their atonement is tragic in the sense that Royce understands it; the deeds that led up to the theft, and the theft itself, cannot be undone. But the character of each, and the relationship that they share, may be made stronger than it would have been had the transgression not occurred. Admittedly, we lack the context of *Analects* 13.18 needed to recommend this reading over and against others. Still, it is plausible that Confucius sees in the Duke of She's "Upright Gong" someone who has acted shamelessly and failed to engage in acts of atonement at a time when doing so is most needed.

CONCLUSION

I have argued in this chapter that there is a strong affinity in conceptions of shame held by Royce, Confucius, and Mencius. I have also argued for an equally strong affinity between notions of atonement from Royce and that present in (or at least are suggested in) the *Analects*. Because Royce so often employs these concepts within theologically framed discussions, it may be tempting to characterize this chapter as implying resonance between Christianity and Confucianism more generally. Although a number of scholars have proposed such compatibility, this has not been my intention.[78] My purpose has been to reveal a shared sensitivity to the problems wrought by wrongdoing, a belief in the capacity of ourselves and others to reform, and a commitment to strengthening individuals and communities in the wake of acts that have been destructive. That said, because Royce borrows so heavily from St. Paul, and because such comparative analyses have often identified Paul as the Christian counterpart to Confucius, what I have put forward in this chapter may very well be of interest to scholars drawn to this connection.

Conclusion

LOOKING BACK

In the chapters of this book, I have illustrated some of the deep affinities between Confucianism and American philosophy, including lines of direct influence in the thought of Emerson and Thoreau, and conceptual compatibility in the thought of Peirce, James, and Royce. My intention has been to expand the scope of this area of comparative philosophy beyond the typically engaged duo of Confucius and Dewey. This approach has been aimed at illustrating the wide breadth of points of contact that can be made between what initially seem to be decidedly disparate traditions, separated by a wide expanse of space and time. I described my project as one in comparative philosophy, and I outlined several reasons why one might engage in comparative philosophy. Taking account of these objectives, let us briefly review the comparative engagements comprising the preceding chapters.

I outlined the following aims of comparative philosophy in the introduction:

- Comparing responses to a philosophical question from more than one tradition gives us more information than we would have if we were to consult only one.

- Comparing philosophical traditions increases our understanding of traditions with which we are less familiar or altogether unfamiliar.
- Comparing philosophical traditions increases our understanding of traditions with which we are more familiar, revealing aspects of the known tradition that went unnoticed.
- Comparative philosophy leads to creative responses to philosophical problems.

Taking stock of the five comparative encounters in this book, it seems that each of these aims is fulfilled.

The philosophical questions asked in this book include: With whom should we be friends? When is civil disobedience justifiable? How should we attain beliefs? Are we naturally moral? How should we act if we have committed wrongdoing? Our answers to each of these questions have been buoyed by the philosophical apparatuses of two traditions and are thus more robust than they would be if buttressed by only one.

Each of these comparative engagements has allowed for greater understanding of the tradition with which the reader is less familiar. Assuming that the reader is not equally fluent in Confucianism and American philosophy, whichever tradition was less known prior to reading this book is likely better known now, thanks to the comparative approach. Assuming that the reader was less familiar with Confucianism, the links with Emerson and Thoreau in chapters 1 and 2 might have proven particularly useful, given their directly engaging with the ideas of Confucius and Mencius. Then again, if the reader were a scholar of James (for example), chapter 4 would have been a logical point of initiation, via the thought of Mencius and Xunzi. Assuming that the reader was less familiar with American philosophy, chapters 1 and 2 might again have been particularly useful, given Emerson's and Thoreau's direct engagement with Confucian texts. Then again, if the reader were a scholar of Xunzi (again, to choose an example), chapter 4 might have been a logical point of initiation, via the thought of James.

Additionally, each of these comparative engagements may very well have revealed to the reader unseen aspects of the more known tradition. Assuming that the reader was more familiar with Confucianism, he or she probably would have had a picture of the type of morality that Confucius and Mencius advocate. He might not have realized, however, the extent to which Confucius and Mencius address the question of how to behave after having committed an act of wrongdoing. In this case, chapter 5 might have been especially revealing. Assuming that the reader was more familiar with American philosophy, he would probably be aware of Peirce's methods of belief fixation. He might not have realized, however, the degree to which Peirce unites the epistemic with the ethical. In this case, chapter 3 might have been particularly suggestive.

Finally, each of these comparative engagements has led to creative solutions to philosophical problems—or at the least, creative approaches. The approaches are creative, at the least, because they combine resources from Confucian and American philosophical traditions. Recalling Angle's set of terms, each chapter has been a performance of "rooted global philosophy," involving "constructive engagement" between two philosophical traditions that are not ordinarily united. It is sometimes remarked that there are no longer any original ideas. If this is true, then creative solutions to perennial questions might be too much for anyone to ask. Still, many readers will find the solutions to the philosophical questions raised in the preceding chapters to be novel and provocative. Even if they carry an air of familiarity, hearing the solutions spoken in new voices may illuminate and inspire as much as hearing them for the first time.

LOOKING AHEAD

It has not been my intention to be comprehensive. Rather, I have hoped to provide in these pages a collection of comparative engagements that are original and diverse, bringing to light connections between Confucian and American philosophers that have previously gone unnoticed or underappreciated and that help us to understand better the thought of each. Certainly, other aspects of the philosophies of those who are discussed in this book could be taken up in comparative analysis. Here I will put forward two examples, allowing the reader to think of others.

Transcendentalists are recognized by many for their attention to the connection of humans with nature, which often takes a spiritual bent. Perhaps this theme might be drawn out in comparison with Confucian ideas about the relationship between humans and *tian* 天. Pragmatists are often identified with James's "pragmatic theory of truth," a doctrine that has perhaps been misunderstood more than it has been understood. Perhaps a comparison of James's theory of knowledge with Confucian notions of thinking (*si* 思), learning (*xue* 學), and knowing (*zhi* 智) would elucidate James's theory while introducing Confucian epistemology to those primarily rooted in American thought.

Likewise, there are several texts and philosophers not discussed in this book that warrant scholarly attention. On the Confucian side, I remained silent about two of the *Four Books*: the *Great Learning* (*Daxue* 大學) and the *Doctrine of the Mean* (*Zhongyong* 中庸). These texts certainly could be brought into comparative engagement with American philosophy, as could the *Classic of Filial Piety* (*Xiaojing* 孝經). Scholars may also consider Neo-Confucians such as Zhu Xi (1130–1200) and Wang Yangming (1472–1529), both of whom contribute significantly to the development of Confucian thought. A sixth chapter might have been devoted to a comparative engagement of Confucianism with the thought of George Santayana (1863–1952), whose penchant for poetry invites connections with Confucian texts, which often make profitable use of the *Odes* (*Shijing* 詩經). Robert W. Smid has given trenchant treatments of the philosophical methods of William Ernest Hocking (1873–1966) and F. S. C. Northrop (1893–1992), American pioneers in comparative philosophy.[1] There is fertile ground for further analysis of the intersections of Confucianism with the thought of each. Some work has been done comparing Confucianism with Neo-Pragmatism, particularly, the thought of Richard Rorty (1931–2007).[2] Other Neo-Pragmatists such as Nelson Goodman (1906–1998), W. V. O. Quine (1908–2000), and Hilary Putnam (1926–2016) are also worth exploring.

Confucian philosophy and American philosophy have a lot to learn from one other. My hope is that scholars of these traditions will continue the conversations that have begun and initiate innovative and productive lines of dialogue. In keeping with this spirit, we are fitly advised by the words of Mencius:

Mencius said to Wan Zhang, "That scholar, whose goodness is most outstanding in the village, will become a friend to all the good scholars of the village. That scholar, whose goodness is most outstanding in the state, will become a friend to all the good scholars of the state. That scholar, whose goodness is the most outstanding in the world, will become a friend to all the good scholars of the world. When he feels that being a friend of all the good scholars of the world is not enough, he will go back in time to consider the people of antiquity, repeating their poems and reading their books. Not knowing what they were like as persons, he considers what they were like in their own time. This is to go back and make friends." (*Mencius* 5B8)

Considering what they were like in their own time, Confucianism and American philosophy confront us as traditions that are worlds apart. A vast expanse of time and space stands between the inceptions of each. At the same time, Confucianism and American philosophy are deeply kindred traditions. Like friends, with due care and mutual understanding, they may enact a bond that is enlivening, enriching, and enduring.

Notes

INTRODUCTION

1. Robert W. Smid, *Methodologies of Comparative Philosophy: The Pragmatist and Process Traditions* (Albany: State University of New York Press, 2009), 2.
2. Ibid. (emphasis in original).
3. For an exemplary survey of this kind, see Tim Connolly, *Doing Philosophy Comparatively* (New York: Bloomsbury, 2015).
4. Stephen C. Angle, *Sagehood: The Contemporary Significance of Neo-Confucian Philosophy* (New York: Oxford University Press, 2009), 6.
5. Ibid.
6. Robert Cummings Neville, *The Highroad Around Modernism* (Albany: State University of New York Press, 1992), 169.
7. Ibid., 171.
8. Ibid., 163.
9. For the earliest survey, see Dale Riepe, *The Philosophy of India and Its Influence on American Thought* (Springfield: Thomas Press, 1970).
10. Philip Goldberg, *American Veda: From Emerson and the Beatles to Yoga and Meditation—How Indian Spirituality Changed the West* (New York: Harmony Books, 2013). Another recent book with a

similar, though not identical, trajectory is Arthur Versluis, *American Gurus: From Transcendentalism to New Age Religion* (New York: Oxford University Press, 2014).

11. See, for instance, Van Meter Ames, *Zen and American Thought* (Honolulu: University of Hawaii Press, 1962); Kenneth K. Inada and Nolan P. Jacobson (eds.), *Buddhism and American Thinkers* (Albany: State University of New York Press, 1984); Rick Fields, *How the Swans Came to the Lake: A Narrative History of Buddhism in America* (Boston: Shambhala, 1992); Steve Odin, *The Social Self in Zen and American Pragmatism* (Albany: State University of New York Press, 1996).

12. Angle, *Sagehood*, 8.

13. For Mead, see especially Odin, *The Social Self in Zen and American Pragmatism*. Odin builds upon the framework of Hall and Ames, *Thinking Through Confucius* (Albany: State University of New York Press, 1987). Hall and Ames return to this point of comparison in *Thinking from the Han: Self, Truth, and Transcendence in Chinese and Western Culture* (Albany: State University of New York Press, 1998), 41–43. For Addams, see Mathew A. Foust, "Perplexities of Filiality: Confucius and Jane Addams on the Private/Public Distinction," *Asian Philosophy* 18, no. 2 (2008): 149–166.

14. Dewey is unique among *Classical* American philosophers in this regard, but he is not the only figure associated with American Pragmatism to visit China. A student of James and Royce, William Ernest Hocking (1873–1966), a second-generation American Pragmatist, led a commission (1930–1932) that visited India, Myanmar (then Burma), China, and Japan over a nine-month period to study the ongoing effects of missionary work in each country. Findings were published in *Re-Thinking Missions: A Layman's Inquiry after One Hundred Years* (New York: Harper and Brothers, 1932). Hocking also published an early comparative study of the Neo-Confucian philosopher Zhu Xi (1130–1200). See Hocking, "Chu Hsi's Theory of Knowledge," *Harvard Journal of Asiatic Studies* 1, no. 1 (1936): 109–127.

15. The most incisive account of Dewey's visit to China and its effects on his subsequent thought is Jessica Ching-sze Wang, *John Dewey*

in China: To Teach and to Learn (Albany: State University of New York Press, 2010).

16. For more on the connections between Dewey and Hu Shih, see Wang, *John Dewey in China*, and Sor-hoon Tan, "China's Pragmatist Experiment in Democracy: Hu Shih's Pragmatism and Dewey's Influence in China," *Metaphilosophy* 35, nos. 1–2 (2004): 44–64.
17. Joseph Grange, *John Dewey, Confucius, and Global Philosophy* (Albany: State University of New York Press), 89.
18. David L. Hall and Roger T. Ames, *The Democracy of the Dead: Dewey, Confucius, and the Hope for Democracy in China* (Chicago and La Salle: Open Court, 1999), 15 (emphasis in original).
19. Ibid., 203.
20. Sor-hoon Tan, *Confucian Democracy: A Deweyan Reconstruction* (Albany: State University of New York Press, 2004), 202.
21. Ibid., 203.
22. Articulations of a Confucian-Deweyan hybrid notion of democracy have not been without their critics. See May Sim, "Dewey and Confucius: On Moral Education," *Journal of Chinese Philosophy* 36, no. 1 (2009): 85–105; David Elstein, "Why Early Confucianism Cannot Generate Democracy," *Dao: A Journal of Comparative Philosophy* 9, no. 4 (2010): 427–443; Russell Shen, "Dissimilarities between Deweyan Pragmatism and Confucianism," *Paideusis* 20, no. 1 (2012): 24–32.
23. Chung-ying Cheng, "Preface," *Journal of Chinese Philosophy* 36, no. 1 (2009): 2 (emphasis in original).
24. For an overview of trends in comparative scholarship between Confucianism and American Pragmatism, see Mathew A. Foust, "Confucianism and American Pragmatism," *Philosophy Compass* 10, no. 6 (2015): 369–378. Some of the content of this introduction duplicates some of the content of that article.
25. Richard Shusterman, "Pragmatism and East-Asian Thought," *Metaphilosophy* 35, nos. 1–2 (2004): 17.
26. Daniel J. Stephens, "Confucianism, Pragmatism, and Socially Beneficial Philosophy," *Journal of Chinese Philosophy* 36, no. 1 (2009): 53.
27. Haiming Wen, *Confucian Pragmatism as the Art of Contextualizing*

Personal Experience and World (Lanham: Lexington Books, 2009), 321.
28. With "broadening a comparative horizon," I echo a phrase that I first used in a special issue of the *Journal of Chinese Philosophy* dedicated to new comparisons between Chinese and American philosophies. See Mathew A. Foust, "Introduction: Chinese and American Philosophies: Broadening a Comparative Horizon," *Journal of Chinese Philosophy* 39, no. 2 (2012): 169–173.
29. For further development of this thesis, see Robert Cummings Neville, "Confucianism as a World Philosophy," *Journal of Chinese Philosophy* 21, no. 1 (1994): 5–25.
30. John Berthrong, "From Xunzi to Boston Confucianism," *Journal of Chinese Philosophy* 30, nos. 3–4 (2003): 433.
31. Similarly, see Degui Cai's discussion of "Hawaiian Confucianism," comprising scholars who have been based at the University of Hawaii. Degui Cai, "Hawaiian Confucianism," *Journal of Chinese Philosophy* 32, no. 1 (2005): 123–138.
32. Berthrong, "From Xunzi to Boston Confucianism," 437.
33. Robert Cummings Neville, *Boston Confucianism: Portable Tradition in the Late-Modern World* (Albany: State University of New York Press, 2000), 21.
34. For further development of this connection, see Neville, "Confucianism as a World Philosophy."
35. Neville, *Boston Confucianism*, 21.
36. Robert Cummings Neville, "Metaphysics and World Philosophy: W. E. Hocking on Chinese Philosophy," in *A William Ernest Hocking Reader*, ed. John Lachs and D. Micah Hester (Nashville: Vanderbilt University Press, 2004), 379n2. Neville has suggested that even Confucianism is not essential to Boston Confucianism: ". . . Boston Confucianism is a form of contemporary philosophic practice, not exclusively or even essentially scholarship about the Confucian tradition" (ibid., 368).
37. Neville, *Boston Confucianism*, 193–209.
38. The Transcendental Club was founded in Cambridge, Massachusetts, on September 8, 1836.
39. For example, see the discussion of *tian* (天) in Roger T. Ames and

Henry Rosemont, Jr., *The Analects of Confucius: A Philosophical Translation* (New York: Ballantine Books, 1998), 46–48. Ames and Rosemont translate *ren* (仁) as "authoritative conduct."
40. Ibid., 48.
41. I will also employ the prevalent Pinyin transliteration of Chinese terms.
42. Egbert S. Oliver, "The Asia in Emerson's Mind," *Korean Survey* 2 (1953): 12.
43. There is evidence suggesting that Emerson read the French translation in question, although he does not appear to have kept a notebook of English translations of passages from it as Thoreau did. A journal entry of 1855 reads: "'Connais les ceremonies. Si tu en penetres le sens tu gouverneras un royaume, avec la meme facilite que tu regards dans ta main.' Confucius." See *Journals and Miscellaneous Notebooks of Ralph Waldo Emerson*, Vol. XIII: 1852–1855, ed. Ralph H. Orth and Alfred R. Ferguson (Cambridge: Belknap Press, 1977), 384.
44. See Jiliang L. Tu (ed.), *The Selected Writings of C. S. Peirce* (Beijing: Publishing House of China's Social Sciences, 2006). For an overview of the current state of Peirce studies in China, see Yi Jiang and Binmin Zhong, "Peirce Studies in China in the 21st Century," *European Journal of Pragmatism and American Philosophy* 6, no. 2 (2014): 252–260.
45. For a previous comparative study of Confucius and Royce, see Mathew A. Foust, "Loyalty in the Teachings of Confucius and Josiah Royce," *Journal of Chinese Philosophy* 39, no. 2 (2012): 192–206.

CHAPTER 1. CONFUCIANISM AND EMERSON

1. *Journals and Miscellaneous Notebooks of Ralph Waldo Emerson*, Vol. II., ed. William H. Gilman, Alfred R. Ferguson, and Merrell R. Davis (Cambridge: Belknap Press, 1961), 378.
2. Joshua Marshman, *The Works of Confucius: Containing the Original Text with a Translation* (Serampore: Mission Press, 1809).

Marshman apparently intended two volumes but produced only this one.

3. For record of the book withdrawal, see *Journals and Miscellaneous Notebooks of Ralph Waldo Emerson*, Vol. VI, ed. Ralph H. Orth (Cambridge: Belknap Press, 1966), 162n246.

4. *Journals and Miscellaneous Notebooks of Ralph Waldo Emerson*, Vol. V, ed. Merton M. Sealts, Jr. (Cambridge: Belknap Press, 1965), 120–122. Marshman divides passages from the *Analects* into numbered sentences, giving commentary on sentences rather than on passages as wholes. Emerson's "Sentences of Confucius" follow Marshman's way of parsing the text.

5. The Four Books are: *Great Learning, Doctrine of the Mean, Analects,* and *Mencius*. Emerson read these in David Collie, *The Chinese Classical Work Commonly Called the Four Books* (Malacca: Mission Press, 1828). Emerson mentions his engagement with this text in correspondence to Margaret Fuller: "I have the best of Chinese Confucian books lately, an octavo published at Malacca, in English." See: Letter to Margaret Fuller, June 7, 1843, *The Letters of Ralph Waldo Emerson*, Vol. III, ed. Ralph L. Rusk (New York: Columbia University Press, 1939), 179.

6. *Journals and Miscellaneous Notebooks of Ralph Waldo Emerson*, Vol. VIII, ed. William H. Gilman and J. E. Parsons (Cambridge: Belknap Press, 1970), 410, 424.

7. The "Ethnical Scriptures" column for April 1843 features "Sayings of Confucius," culled from Marshman's translation of the *Analects*. The "Ethnical Scriptures" column for October 1843 features quotes from the "Chinese Four Books," culled from Collie's translation. See *The Dial: A Magazine for Literature, Philosophy, and Religion*, Vol. III (393–394) and Vol. IV (205–210) (New York: Russell & Russell, 1961 [1843]).

8. James Legge, *Confucian Analects, the Great Learning, and the Doctrine of the Mean: The Chinese Classics I* (London: Trübner, 1861). In a letter to Charles H. Glover, dated October 16, 1863, Emerson "apologizes for his delay in returning a stately edition of Confucius and adds that he many years ago knew the substance of this work not only in Marshman" but also "in [Collie's] *The Chinese Classical*

Work, published at Malacca." As Ralph L. Rusk correctly infers, "The book Emerson was returning was no doubt James Legge's translation." See: *The Letters of Ralph Waldo Emerson*, Vol. V, ed. Ralph. L. Rusk (New York: Columbia University Press, 1939), 338.

9. *Journals and Miscellaneous Notebooks of Ralph Waldo Emerson*, Vol. XV, ed. Linda Allardt, David W. Hill, and Ruth H. Bennett (Cambridge: Belknap Press, 1982), 362.
10. Ralph Waldo Emerson, *Representative Men and Miscellanies* (Boston and New York: Houghton Mifflin Company, 1921), 472–473.
11. This situation may now be changing. See, for instance, Kyle Bryant Simmons, "Emerson, the American Confucius: An Exploration of Confucian Motifs in the Early Writings (1830–1843) of Ralph Waldo Emerson" (PhD Dissertation, University of Texas at Dallas, 2013); Neal Dolan and Laura Jane Wey, "Emerson and China," and Mathew A. Foust, "Confucius and Emerson on the Virtue of Self-Reliance," in *A Power to Translate the World: New Essays on Emerson and International Culture*, ed. David LaRocca and Ricardo Miguel-Alfonso (Lebanon: University Press of New England, 2015), 236–248 and 249–261. For a recent comparison of Emerson's thought with Neo-Confucianism, see Yoshio Takanashi, *Emerson and Neo-Confucianism: Crossing Paths Over the Pacific* (New York: Palgrave Macmillan, 2014).
12. John Jay Chapman, *Emerson, and Other Essays* (New York: AMS Press, 1965 [1899]), 18.
13. John S. Harrison, *The Teachers of Emerson* (New York: Sturgis & Walton, 1910), 279.
14. Frederic Ives Carpenter, *Emerson and Asia* (Cambridge: Harvard University Press, 1931), 234.
15. Carl T. Jackson, *The Oriental Religions and American Thought: Nineteenth-Century Explorations* (Westport: Greenwood Press, 1981), 53.
16. Ibid., 55.
17. Richard Grossman, *The Tao of Emerson: The Wisdom of the Tao Te Ching as Found in the Words of Ralph Waldo Emerson* (New York: The Modern Library, 2007), xxiv. Grossman does not clarify the

meaning of Emerson's phrase "the infinitude of the Asiatic soul," nor does he clarify the significance of this purported link between Confucius and Emerson. I am less sure that Confucius "believed in" "the infinitude of the Asiatic soul," given the cluster of abstract concepts at work in this phrase (infinitude, Asiatic, soul).

18. Ibid., xxiv.
19. Lin Yutang, *The Wisdom of India and China* (New York: The Modern Library, 1942), 569.
20. Arthur Christy, *The Orient in Transcendentalism: A Study of Emerson, Thoreau, and Alcott* (New York: Octagon Books, 1963 [1932]), 123.
21. Simmons, "Emerson, the American Confucius," 6.
22. Marshman, *The Works of Confucius*, 36. Marshman offers the following comment on the quote: "*Moo* is an adverb of prohibition. *Yaou*, a friend; properly one who assists another in virtue. 'Unlike yourself.' Such a friend would not improve, but injure you" (ibid.).
23. *Analects* 9.25 is a duplicate of the second half of 1.8.
24. Marshman, *The Works of Confucius*, 33–37.
25. Ralph Waldo Emerson, "Society," in *The Early Lectures of Ralph Waldo Emerson*, Vol. II, ed. Stephen E. Whicher, Robert E. Spiller, and Wallace E. Williams (Cambridge: Belknap Press, 1964), 104.
26. Ibid., 104–105. Emerson's quote of Confucius is from Marshman, *The Works of Confucius*.
27. Ibid., 105.
28. Literally, "ruler's son" or "noble son," often translated as "gentleman," "superior man," or "noble man," the *junzi* (君子) is a moral exemplar.
29. Edward Slingerland, *Confucius Analects: With Selections from Traditional Commentaries* (Indianapolis: Hackett, 2003), 1.
30. Eric C. Mullis, "Confucius and Aristotle on the Goods of Friendship," *Dao: A Journal of Comparative Philosophy* 9, no. 4 (2010): 395.
31. Sor-hoon Tan, "Mentor or Friend? Confucius and Aristotle on Equality and Ethical Development in Friendship," *International Studies in Philosophy* 33, no. 4 (2001): 115.
32. *Mencius* 3A4.
33. As Tan explains, David L. Hall and Roger T. Ames suggest that

peng (朋) is the inferior friend and *you* (友) is the superior friend, but the sequence of the terms in *pengyou* suggests the reverse, particularly if this relationship is analogous to the elder brother (*xiong* 兄)–younger brother (*di* 弟) relationship (*xiongdi* 兄弟), in which the superior party appears first (Tan, "Mentor or Friend?," 114).

34. Tim Connolly, "Friendship and Filial Piety: Relational Ethics in Aristotle and Early Confucianism," *Journal of Chinese Philosophy* 39, no. 1 (2012): 82.
35. Mullis, "Confucius and Aristotle on the Goods of Friendship," 394.
36. Tan, "Mentor or Friend?," 116.
37. David L. Hall and Roger T. Ames, *Thinking from the Han* (Albany: State University of New York Press, 1989), 261.
38. Ibid., 260.
39. Xiufen Lu, "Rethinking Confucian Friendship," *Asian Philosophy* 20, no. 3 (2010): 235.
40. Literally, "way," "direction," or "road," in the *Analects*, *dao* (道) refers to the Confucian path of moral cultivation.
41. Slingerland, *Confucius Analects*, 137.
42. The rhetorical style of *Analects* 16.4 is much like that of *Analects* 9.30 (discussed next) and *Analects* 1.1 (discussed earlier) insofar as each utterance from Confucius takes the form of a triplet. There are numerous occasions upon which Confucius gives lists of three, which undoubtedly carry mnemonic efficacy for the disciples.
43. Whalen Lai, "Friendship in Confucian China: Classical and Late Ming," in *Friendship East and West: Philosophical Perspectives*, ed. Oliver Leaman (Surrey: Curzon, 1995), 220.
44. Slingerland, *Confucius Analects*, 97.
45. In this passage, too, the examples are three in number.
46. Recall *Analects* 12.23.
47. Russell B. Goodman, "Emerson and Skepticism: A Reading of 'Friendship,'" *European Journal of Pragmatism and American Philosophy* 2, no. 2 (2010): 9.
48. George Sebouhian, "A Dialogue with Death: An Examination of Emerson's 'Friendship,'" *Studies in the American Renaissance* (1989): 235.

49. Christopher J. Newfield, "Loving Bondage: Emerson's Ideal Relationships," *ATQ* 5, no. 3 (1991): 187.
50. Ralph Waldo Emerson, "Friendship," in *Essays & Poems*, ed. Joel Porte, Harold Bloom, and Paul Kane (New York: Library of America, 1996), 341.
51. Ibid.
52. Ibid.
53. Ibid.
54. Ibid., 342.
55. Ibid.
56. Ibid.
57. Ibid.
58. Ibid.
59. Ibid., 343.
60. Ibid.
61. Ibid., 345.
62. Ibid., 350.
63. Ibid., 348.
64. Ibid., 346.
65. Ibid., 348.
66. *Book of Common Prayer*, http://www.bcponline.org/, accessed 27 September 2015.
67. Emerson, "Friendship," 349.
68. Ibid., 342.
69. Ibid., 341.
70. Ibid., 343.
71. Ibid.
72. Ibid., 352.
73. Ibid., 351.
74. Ibid., 350.
75. Todd Lekan expresses a similar sentiment about Emerson's account: "On the one hand, some degree of idealization is necessary for friendships to grow beyond their embryonic forms. Moreover, true friends model impersonal values and for that they deserve some degree of idealization. On the other hand, Emersonian friends recognize that even those friends whose excellences they most admire are only partial embodiments of ideals. Is it possible to sustain

these friendships, at least without a certain kind of self-deceptive 'double-consciousness'?" See Todd Lekan, "Appreciating the Impersonal in Emerson (That's What Friends Are For)," *Journal of Speculative Philosophy* 21, no. 2 (2007): 101.
76. Emerson, "Friendship," 354.
77. The translation is from Ames and Rosemont. Slingerland renders Confucius's response, "To bring comfort to the aged, to inspire trust in my friends, and be cherished by the youth." That Confucius aspires *to cherish* the youth rather than *be cherished by* the youth seems more consistent with the other-centered nature of the first two aspirations.
78. Emerson, "Friendship," 352.
79. Ibid., 354.

CHAPTER 2. CONFUCIANISM AND THOREAU

1. For general treatments of the Asian resonances in Thoreau, see: Arthur Christy, *The Orient in American Transcendentalism: A Study of Emerson, Thoreau and Alcott* (New York: Octagon Books, 1963), 186–233; Alan D. Hodder, *Thoreau's Ecstatic Witness* (New Haven: Yale University Press, 2001), 174–217 ("The Artist of Kouroo"); David Scott, "Rewalking Thoreau and Asia: 'Light from the East' for 'A Very Yankee Sort of Oriental,'" *Philosophy East & West* 57, no. 1 (2007): 14–39. For Daoist resonances in Thoreau, see David T. Y. Chen, "Thoreau and Taoism," in *Asian Response to American Literature*, ed. C. D. Narasimhaiah (New York: Barnes & Noble, 1972), 406–416; Gary Simon, "What Henry David Thoreau Didn't Know about Lao Tzu: Taoist Parallels in Thoreau," *Literature East and West* 16 (1973): 253–271; John Emerson, "Thoreau's Construction of Taoism," *Thoreau Journal Quarterly* 12, no. 2 (1980): 5–9; Aimin Cheng, "Humanity as 'A Part and Parcel of Nature': A Comparative Study of Thoreau's and Taoist Concepts of Nature," in *Thoreau's Sense of Place: Essays in American Environmental Writing*, ed. Richard J. Schneider (Iowa City: University of Iowa Press, 2000), 207–220.
2. For Confucian resonances in Thoreau, see Lyman V. Cady,

"Thoreau's Quotations from the Confucian Books in *Walden*," *American Literature* 33, no. 1 (1961): 20–32; Hongbo Tan, "Confucius at Walden Pond: Thoreau's Unpublished Confucian Translations," in *Studies in the American Renaissance*, ed. Joel Myerson (Charlottesville: University Press of Virginia, 1993), 275–303.

3. Christy, *The Orient in American Transcendentalism*, 196.
4. Cady, "Thoreau's Quotations from the Confucian Books in *Walden*," 31.
5. Tan, "Confucius at Walden Pond," 287.
6. Jean-Pierre Guillaume Pauthier, *Confucius et Mencius: Les Quatres Livres de Philosophie Morale et Politique de la Chine* (Paris: Charpentier, 1840); Jean-Pierre Guillaume Pauthier, *Les Livres Sacrés de l'Orient* (Paris: Société du Panthéon Littéraire, 1841).
7. Tan, "Confucius at Walden Pond," 285. The "Commonplace Book" is archived in the Berg Collection of English and American Literature at the New York Public Library. These passages are struck through with a light vertical line in pencil, perhaps indicating their having been used by Thoreau in some context(s).
8. The essay was first published in Elizabeth Peabody's *Aesthetic Papers* in 1849 under the title "Resistance to Civil Government." It was included as "Civil Disobedience" in Thoreau's *A Yankee in Canada, with Anti-Slavery and Reform Papers*, published four years after Thoreau's death, in 1866, by Ticknor and Fields. It is thus not quite correct to match "Civil Disobedience" with the year 1849. Because the essay is most known by this title, however, and because the content of the essay remains the same as in the original publication, I use the title most familiar to readers.
9. Tan totals the number of identified passages at twenty-seven, perhaps not counting the unpublished manuscript fragment (Tan, "Confucius at Walden Pond," 285). Tan fully transcribes the passage (*Analects* 11.26) from the unpublished manuscript fragment (Tan, "Confucius at Walden Pond," 298–299).
10. Scholars generally agree that the second drafts of these writings were completed in 1849 (Tan, "Confucius at Walden Pond," 301).
11. Based on various strands of evidence, Tan makes a compelling case for late 1843 as the time of Thoreau's translations (Tan, "Confucius at Walden Pond," 286).

12. Henry David Thoreau, *Civil Disobedience, Solitude and Life Without Principle* (Amherst: Prometheus Books, 1998 [1849]).
13. Ibid., 31.
14. It is not clear whom, precisely, Confucius is advising in *Analects* 8.13. It could be that the advice is intended for all persons, though it might also be that it is advice for those who would govern: "The Master said, 'Be sincerely trustworthy and love learning, and hold fast to the good *dao* (道) until death. Do not enter a state that is endangered, and do not reside in a state that is disordered. If the *dao* is being realized in the world then show yourself; if it is not, then go into reclusion. In a state that has the *dao*, to be poor and of low status is a cause for shame; in a state that is without the *dao*, to be wealthy and honored is equally a cause for shame.'" If the advice is intended for those who would govern, the implication of the sentences quoted by Thoreau may be that it is shameful to allow the citizenry to be poor and of low status when the *dao* prevails and that it is shameful to allow the citizenry to be wealthy and honored when the *dao* does not prevail.
15. Thoreau, *Civil Disobedience*, 44.
16. See, for instance, Lin Yutang, *The Wisdom of America* (New York: The John Day Company, 1950), 190; Scott, "Rewalking Thoreau and Asia," 24.
17. Tan, "Confucius at Walden Pond," 294.
18. Edward H. Madden and Peter H. Hare, "Reflections on Civil Disobedience," *Journal of Value Inquiry* 4, no. 2 (1970): 90.
19. Ibid., 85.
20. Ibid.
21. Thoreau, *Civil Disobedience*, 13.
22. Ibid., 15.
23. Granted, more immediately apparent is a resemblance between Daoist thought about governing and Thoreau's thought about governing. Earlier I cited scholarship addressing this affinity, but it is worth quoting from *Daodejing* 60: "Bringing proper order to a great state is like cooking a small fish." The implication is that only a light touch is needed. Roger T. Ames and David L. Hall, *Daodejing: A Philosophical Translation* (New York: Ballantine Books, 2003).

24. Throughout, I have modified Slingerland's translation by not capitalizing, as he does, the *v* in "virtue."
25. Thoreau, *Walden; or, Life in the Woods* (New York: Dover, 1995 [1854]), 112.
26. The two different senses of "*zheng*" are intended as wordplay. See Ames and Rosemont, *The Analects of Confucius*, 251n201.
27. Tan, "Confucius at Walden Pond," 290. Most current translations render the name of this disciple of Confucius's "Zijian."
28. See also *Analects* 2.1 ("One who rules through the power of virtue is analogous to the Pole Star . . ."), *Analects* 4.25 ("Virtue is never solitary; it always has neighbors"—quoted by Thoreau in "Solitude" in *Walden*), *Analects* 13.16 ("[Act so that] those near to you are pleased, and those who are far from you are drawn closer"), *Analects* 15.5 ("Is Shun not an example of someone who ruled by means of *wu-wei*?"), and so on.
29. Thoreau, *Civil Disobedience*, 18, 19, 20, 21, 23, 26–29, 38, and 42–43.
30. Ibid., 14, 19, 20, 23, and 28–29.
31. Ibid., 28.
32. Ibid., 14.
33. Ibid.
34. *Analects* 5.13: "Zigong said, 'The Master's cultural brilliance is something that is readily heard about, whereas one does not get to hear the Master expounding upon the subjects of human nature or the Way of Heaven.'" This passage is discussed in chapter 4.
35. Above "Koung-tou-tseu" is Thoreau's note in pencil "not C" (Tan, "Confucius at Walden Pond," 303n165). Most current translations render the name of this disciple of Mencius's "Gongduzi."
36. Tan, "Confucius at Walden Pond," 295.
37. Thoreau, *Civil Disobedience*, 30.
38. Ibid., 31. Thoreau cannot be referring to *his* children, as he had none.
39. Ibid., 16.
40. Ibid.
41. Patrick K. Dooley, "Thoreau on Civil Disobedience: From Pacifism to Violence," *Journal of Thought* 13, no. 3 (1978): 182.

42. Peter Singer, *Democracy and Disobedience* (Oxford: Clarendon Press, 1973), 95.
43. Ibid., 95–96.
44. Ames and Rosemont, *The Analects of Confucius*. Slingerland's translation states that the *junzi* has "no predispositions for or against any person." In my view, the broader scope in Ames and Rosemont's translation (anything, rather than any person) is more accurate.
45. See, for instance, *Analects* 3.3, in which Confucius asks rhetorically, "A man who is not *ren*—what has he to do with ritual?"
46. Thoreau, *Civil Disobedience*, 25.
47. The brackets are Thoreau's, with "<degrade>" and "<abase>" in pencil. Most current translations render "Thsi" as "Qin" and "Tchao-meng" as "Zhao Meng."
48. Thoreau, *Civil Disobedience*, 20.
49. Ames and Rosemont, *The Analects of Confucius*. Slingerland translates Confucius's answer: "He first expresses his views, and then acts in accordance with them," however Ames and Rosemont seem to give a more accurate rendering of the sequence of action and speech. In either case, the bonding of word and action is significant.
50. Thoreau, *Civil Disobedience*, 32.
51. Viren Murthy, "The Democratic Potential of Confucian *Minben* Thought," *Asian Philosophy* 10, no. 1 (2000): 34.
52. Ames and Rosemont, *The Analects of Confucius*. Slingerland's translation has "wealthy" in place of "prosperous," but the common association of wealth with money leads me to resist this translation. The broad connotations of "prosperity" are more suitable, as the intended meaning is more centered on sustenance and flourishing than it is on collection of material goods.
53. Justin Tiwald, "A Right of Rebellion in the *Mengzi*?," *Dao: A Journal of Comparative Philosophy* 7, no. 3 (2008): 270.
54. The translation is Bloom's; the bracketed insertion is mine.
55. For more on the ineffectiveness of Zilu and Ran Qiu as ministers, see *Analects* 16.1.
56. The translation is Bloom's; the bracketed insertions are mine.

57. Thoreau, *Civil Disobedience*, 27.
58. Ames and Rosemont render this state of inclination as 'having a taste for' defying authority. In each translation, a fondness for defying authority is being referred to, which a filial person is said to be unlikely to develop.

CHAPTER 3. CONFUCIANISM AND PEIRCE

1. Shanruo Ning Zhang, *Confucianism in Contemporary Chinese Politics: An Actionable Account of Authoritarian Political Culture* (Lanham: Lexington Books, 2016).
2. Sor-hoon Tan, "Authoritative Master Kong (Confucius) in an Authoritarian Age," *Dao: A Journal of Comparative Philosophy* 9, no. 2 (2010): 137–149.
3. Charles S. Peirce, "The Fixation of Belief," in *Charles S. Peirce: Selected Writings (Values in a Universe of Chance)*, ed. Philip P. Wiener (New York: Dover, 1958), 99.
4. Ibid., 100.
5. *Analects* 5.28.
6. *Analects* 7.17.
7. Slingerland, *Confucius Analects*, 9.
8. Paula S. Rothenberg, "Peirce's Defense of the Scientific Method," *Journal of the History of Philosophy* 13, no. 4 (1975): 484.
9. Peirce, "The Fixation of Belief," 101.
10. Ibid., 102.
11. Ibid.
12. Ibid. (emphasis in original).
13. Ibid.
14. Ibid., 103.
15. Ibid.
16. Ibid.
17. Ibid.
18. Ibid., 105.
19. Ibid.
20. Ibid., 106.

21. Ibid.
22. Ibid.
23. Ibid., 107.
24. Ibid., 107–108.
25. Ibid., 107.
26. The phrase "or would be the same if inquiry were sufficiently persisted in" is often inserted in reproductions of "The Fixation of Belief," with editors of Peirce's *Collected Papers* having drawn from an unidentified manuscript they date 1903. For more on this, see Charles S. Peirce, "The Fixation of Belief," in *Charles S. Peirce: Illustrations of the Logic of Science*, ed. Cornelis de Waal (Chicago: Open Court, 2014), 67.
27. Peirce, "The Fixation of Belief," in Wiener, ed., *Charles S. Peirce: Selected Writings*, 111.
28. Ibid.
29. It is not altogether clear what it is for a belief to be "fixed" or stable, other than its being accompanied by a feeling of relief from the irritation of doubt. For an exploration of this question, see Jeff Kasser, "How Settled Are Settled Beliefs in 'The Fixation of Belief'?," *Transactions of the Charles S. Peirce Society* 47, no. 2 (2011): 226–247.
30. For a treatment of "The Fixation of Belief" that gives due credit to this aspect, see John Kaag, "Peirce and Plato on the Fixation of Belief," *Transactions of the Charles S. Peirce Society* 48, no. 4 (2012): 512–529.
31. Tim Connolly, "Fallibilism in Early Confucian Philosophy," Peirce's Philosophy and Chinese Philosophy Session, Charles S. Peirce Centennial Congress, University of Massachusetts–Lowell, July 16, 2014 (unpublished paper).
32. Translations of the title of the *Shijing* include the *Odes*, the *Book of Songs* and the *Book of Poems*.
33. See, for instance, *Analects* 3.14, 4.22, 8.1, 8.19, and 8.20.
34. See, for instance, *Analects* 7.18, 8.8, 16.13, 17.9, and 17.10.
35. See, for instance, *Analects* 3.9, 3.10, 3.11, 3.26, and 6.25.
36. Herbert Fingarette, "How the *Analects* Portrays the Ideal of Efficacious Authority," *Journal of Chinese Philosophy* 8, no.1 (1981): 29.

37. Tan, "Authoritative Master Kong (Confucius) in an Authoritarian Age," 139.
38. *Analects* 7.33.
39. *Analects* 7.34.
40. See, for instance, *Analects* 11.22, in which Confucius gives contradictory responses to the same question from Ranyou (whom he seeks to urge on) and Zilu (whom he seeks to rein in).
41. At least one scholar would emphasize my claim that there is no hint of the method of authority *here*, holding that the *Analects* "reflects a specific construction of Confucius confronting contingency," while other texts, such as the appendices to the *Book of Changes* and the *Mencius*, portray Confucius as a "central authority." See Joachim Gentz, "Confucius Confronting Contingency in the *Lunyu* and the *Gongyang Zhuan*," *Journal of Chinese Philosophy* 39, no. 1 (2012): 63, 60.
42. *Analects* 11.4.
43. The expression "Great minds think alike" is brought to mind.
44. See, for instance, *Analects* 5.9, in which Zigong contrasts himself with Yan Hui; the former learns one thing and thereby understands two, while Yan Hui learns one thing and thereby understands ten. See also *Analects* 6.3 in which Confucius singles out Yan Hui as the only person whom he has met who has truly loved learning.
45. In comments on a draft of this chapter, Andrew Lambert says of *Analects* 15.36, "Sounds pretty tenacious to me!" Propositional attitudes taking the form of "I will never do *x*" undoubtedly do sound tenacious, but I take it that in this case, what one is supposed to never do is relinquish one's capacity for critical thinking—exactly that which is done when adopting the method of tenacity.
46. Ames and Rosemont, *The Analects of Confucius*. The use of "realize" seems to more fully capture that which Slingerland renders as "understand." To "realize" implies both to understand and to embody in action.
47. Granted, merely associating with those he considers right could be construed as an outcome of the *a priori* method of belief fixation.

If so, it would seem this would be a favorable instance of belief fixation via the *a priori* method.
48. This sentiment finds expression again in *Analects* 15.28: "The Master said, 'When the multitude hates a person, you must examine them and judge for yourself. The same holds true for someone whom the multitude love.'"
49. *Analects* 10.24.
50. Ames and Rosemont, *The Analects of Confucius*, 128.
51. *Analects* 6.11.
52. Also see *Analects* 5.15.
53. Angle, *Sagehood*, 61.
54. Peirce writes that there is "one corollary which itself deserves to be inscribed upon every wall of the city of philosophy: Do not block the way of inquiry." Quoted in Susan Haack, "Do Not Block the Way of Inquiry," *Transactions of the Charles S. Peirce Society* 50, no. 3 (2014): 319.
55. T. L. Short, "Peirce on the Aim of Inquiry: Another Reading of 'Fixation,'" *Transactions of the Charles S. Peirce Society* 36, no. 1 (2000): 3.
56. Ibid., 4.
57. As we have seen, Confucius defers to the authoritativeness of the sage-kings, but this is not the same as adopting belief via the method of authority as Peirce describes it.
58. Peirce, "The Fixation of Belief," in Weiner, ed., *Charles S. Peirce: Selected Writings*, 111.

CHAPTER 4. CONFUCIANISM AND JAMES

1. Slingerland, *Confucius Analects*, 200.
2. Fung Yu-lan, *A History of Chinese Philosophy*, Vol. 1 (Princeton: Princeton University Press, 1952 [1934]), 281.
3. Paul Rakita Goldin, *Rituals of the Way: The Philosophy of Xunzi* (Chicago and La Salle: Open Court, 1999), 11.
4. Ibid., 12.
5. James Behuniak calls this Mencius's "botanical model of moral

development" and discusses several passages throughout the *Mencius* in which Mencius incorporates these metaphors. See James Behuniak Jr., *Mencius on Becoming Human* (Albany: State University of New York Press, 2005), 37–41. According to Behuniak, "Cultivating the person is likened to growing a tree. It involves an accretion of feeling and behavior that reinforces and enlarges a pattern of growth over the span of a life" (40).

6. There are several other passages concerning the bad faith of claiming that one is (or one's ruler is) incapable of doing what is morally demanding. See, for example, *Mencius* 4A1 and 4A11. When Mencius imagines one making such an evaluation of one's ruler, he likely has in mind as the evaluating subject a minister. Given the nature of the obligations of a minister to a ruler (as discussed in chapter 2), such an evaluation could be as much an indictment of oneself as it is of one's ruler.

7. *Xunzi* (§23, 166). Watson's "prejudiced" connotes partiality in general. For the claim that this argument from Xunzi "is more properly construed as a distinction within moral discourse," see A. S. Cua, "The Conceptual Aspect of Hsün-Tzu's Philosophy of Human Nature," *Philosophy East and West* 27, no. 4 (1977): 378.

8. Donald J. Munro, *The Concept of Man in Early China* (Stanford: Stanford University Press, 1969), 78 (emphasis in original).

9. *Xunzi* (§23, 165–166).

10. Goldin, *Rituals of the Way*, 17.

11. Such a stance is more consistent with Daoism, and although Daoism seems to be among Xunzi's influences, it is evidently not so with respect to this aspect of his thought.

12. *Xunzi* (§19, 95).

13. David B. Wong, "Xunzi on Moral Motivation," in *Chinese Language, Thought, and Culture: Nivison and His Critics*, ed. Philip J. Ivanhoe (Chicago and La Salle: Open Court, 1996): 217.

14. Goldin, "Xunzi's Piety," in *Confucian Spirituality*, Vol. 1, ed. Tu Weiming and Mary Evelyn Tucker (New York: Crossroad, 2003), 293 (emphasis in original). Goldin continues, "The rituals of the sage-kings conform to the natural order, and augment it, by confirming the distinctions that man is bound to make by nature. This

is why there is only one set of legitimate rituals. There is only one Way. The sage-kings apprehended it, and their rituals embody it. There is no other Way, and no other constellation of rituals that conforms to the Way" (294).
15. A. S. Cua, "The Quasi-Empirical Aspect of Hsün-Tzu's Philosophy of Human Nature," *Philosophy East and West* 28, no. 1 (1978): 15.
16. Goldin, *Rituals of the Way*, 36–37.
17. Merle Curti, *Human Nature in American Thought: A History* (Madison: University of Wisconsin Press, 1980), 210–211.
18. Ibid., 203.
19. William James, *The Varieties of Religious Experience: A Study in Human Nature* (London and New York: Routledge, 2002 [1902]), 73.
20. Ibid., 106.
21. Ibid., 108.
22. Ibid., 73.
23. Ibid., 75.
24. Quoted in ibid., 95.
25. Curti, *Human Nature in American Thought*, 207.
26. William James, "The Moral Equivalent of War," in *The Works of William James: Essays in Religion and Morality*, ed. Frederick Burkhardt and Fredson Bowers (Cambridge: Harvard University Press, 1982), 171 (emphasis in original).
27. In 1903, Jane Addams gave a lecture titled "A Moral Substitute for War." That James's (later) title is similar to her (earlier) title is more than coincidental. James and Addams appeared together on the same platform at the Thirteenth Universal Peace Congress in 1904 and gave credit to one another in print and correspondence. For a detailed account of the exchange between Addams and James, see Allen F. Davis, *American Heroine: The Life and Legend of Jane Addams* (New York: Oxford University Press, 1973).
28. James, "The Moral Equivalent of War," in *The Works of William James*, 171–172.
29. Ibid., 164.
30. Ibid.
31. William James, "The Moral Philosopher and the Moral Life," in

The Will to Believe and Other Essays in Popular Philosophy (New York: Dover, 1956 [1897]), 211.
32. Ibid.
33. Ibid.
34. Ibid., 213.
35. This is not to suggest that Xunzi and James are identical on this count. Unlike Xunzi, James ties moral strenuousness to religiosity: "The capacity of the strenuous mood lies so deep down among our natural human possibilities that even if there were no metaphysical or traditional grounds for believing in a God, men would postulate one simply as a pretext for living hard, and getting out of the game of existence its keenest possibilities of zest. Our attitude towards concrete evils is entirely different in a world where we believe there are none but finite demanders, from what it is in one where we joyously face tragedy for an infinite demanders' sake. Every sort of energy and endurance, of courage and capacity for handling life's evils, is set free in those who have religious faith" (ibid.).
36. In "Attention," one of his *Talks to Teachers*, James makes the same point, only in this context the remark is about what a teacher must do to arouse the attention of the pupil: "Let him [the teacher] still awaken whatever sources of interest in the subject he can by stirring up connections between it and the pupil's nature, whether in the line of theoretic curiosity, of personal interest, or of pugnacious impulse. The laws of mind will then bring enough pulses of effort into play to keep the pupil exercised in the direction of the subject. There is, in fact, no greater school of effort than the steady struggle to attend to immediately repulsive or difficult objects of thought which have grown to interest us through their association as means, with some remote ideal end." William James, *Talks to Teachers on Psychology and to Students on Some of Life's Ideals* (New York: Henry Holt and Company, 1904 [1899]), 110–111.
37. Bryan W. Van Norden, "Mengzi and Xunzi: Two Views of Human Agency," *International Philosophical Quarterly* 32, no. 2 (1992): 183.
38. James, "What Makes a Life Significant," in *Talks to Teachers on*

Psychology and to Students on Some of Life's Ideals, 275 (emphasis in original).
39. Ibid., 272.
40. Ibid., 272–273.
41. Ibid., 272.

CHAPTER 5. CONFUCIANISM AND ROYCE

1. See, for example, Margaret Urban Walker, *Moral Repair: Reconstructing Moral Relations after Wrongdoing* (Cambridge: Cambridge University Press, 2006) and Linda Radzik, *Making Amends: Atonement in Morality, Law and Politics* (Oxford: Oxford University Press, 2011).
2. Lee H. Yearley, "Virtues and Religious Virtues in the Confucian Tradition," in *Confucian Spirituality*, Volume One, ed. Tu Weiming and Mary Evelyn Tucker (New York: Crossroad, 2003), 145.
3. See Mathew A. Foust, "Nitobe and Royce: Bushidō and the Philosophy of Loyalty," *Philosophy East and West* 65, no. 4 (2015): 1174–1193.
4. Josiah Royce, *The Philosophy of Loyalty* (Nashville: Vanderbilt University Press, 1995 [1908]), 35.
5. Inazo Nitobe, *Bushido: The Soul of Japan* (New York: Dover, 2004 [1900]), 13.
6. Ibid.
7. Ibid., 46.
8. Wolfram Eberhard, *Guilt and Sin in Traditional China* (Berkeley and Los Angeles: University of California Press, 1967), 15.
9. Ibid., 12.
10. "atonement, n.," OED Online, September 2015, Oxford University Press, http://www.oed.com/view/Entry/12599?redirectedFrom=atonement, accessed 27 September 2015.
11. "My efforts to grasp and to expound the 'religion of loyalty' have at length led me, in this book, to views concerning the essence of Christianity such that, if they have any truth, they need to

be carefully considered. For they are, in certain essential respects, novel views; and they concern the central life-problems of all of us." Josiah Royce, *The Problem of Christianity* (Washington, DC: Catholic University of America Press, 2001 [1913]), 38. Given its not being confined to a Christian (or any particular theological) framework, I concur with Kelly A. Parker, who asserts of Royce, "His visionary concept of atonement is especially compelling, pointing as it does toward a practical and constructive role for philosophy in society." Kelly A. Parker, "Atonement and Eidetic Extinction," in *Josiah Royce for the Twenty-First Century*, ed. Kelly A. Parker and Krzysztof Piotr Skowronski (Lanham: Lexington Books, 2012), 213.

12. For a treatment of Royce's ethics that acknowledges the important role played by his moral psychology, see Peter Fuss, *The Moral Philosophy of Josiah Royce* (Cambridge: Harvard University Press, 1965).
13. Josiah Royce, *The Conception of God* (Bristol: Thoemmes Press, 2000 [1897]), 281.
14. In a brief discussion of shame in a book published soon after *The Conception of God*, Royce reiterates this point. See Josiah Royce, *Studies of Good and Evil* (New York: D. Appleton and Company, 1902 [1898]), 188.
15. Josiah Royce, *The Sources of Religious Insight* (New York: Charles Scribner's Sons, 1912), 66.
16. Ibid.
17. Ibid., 66–67.
18. Josiah Royce, *The World and the Individual*, Second Series (New York: Dover, [1901] 1959), 58.
19. Ibid., 59.
20. Ibid. (emphasis in original).
21. Ibid., 359 (emphasis in original).
22. Ibid., 358 (emphasis in original).
23. In Royce's words, "The former lectures emphasized the World; the present course shall be directed towards an understanding of the Human Individual. The previous discussion dealt with the Theory of Being; the aim of what is to come shall be a doctrine about Life" (ibid., 4).

24. For more on Royce and sin, see my "Tragedy and the Sorrow of Finitude: Reflections on Sin and Death in the Philosophy of Josiah Royce," *The Pluralist* 2, no. 2 (2007): 106–114.
25. Royce, *The World and the Individual*, Second Series, 66.
26. Jane Geaney, "Guarding Moral Boundaries: Shame in Early Confucianism," *Philosophy East and West* 54, no. 2 (2004): 120.
27. Bongrae Seok, "Moral Psychology of Shame in Early Confucian Philosophy," *Frontiers of Philosophy in China* 10, no. 1 (2015): 31. The bracketed insertion is mine.
28. In other passages, Confucius expresses pride in disciples who are not ashamed despite undergoing these exact conditions. See *Analects* 9.27 (Zilu's shabby clothing) and 6.11 (Yan Hui's meager rations).
29. For a similar remark, see *Analects* 14.20.
30. It is possible that poor clothing would be a good reason for shame, if poor clothing were a violation of *li* in some circumstance. Paired with "meager rations," however, it is evident that the shame referred to here is coming from poverty. The scholar-official, guided by the *dao*, ought not be perturbed by these superficialities.
31. In *Analects* 5.15, Confucius praises Kong Wenzi for not being ashamed to ask advice from his inferiors. Such shame would have been bad; its absence in Kong Wenzi resulted in his being posthumously accorded the title "Cultured."
32. Nathaniel F. Barrett, "A Confucian Theory of Shame," *Sophia* 54, no. 2 (2015): 155.
33. Ibid., 148.
34. For a study of the ideal of harmony in Confucian thought, see Chenyang Li, *The Confucian Philosophy of Harmony* (New York: Routledge, 2014).
35. See *Analects* 5.5 for Confucius's scathing commentary on "eloquence" (i.e., having "a clever tongue").
36. See also *Analects* 7.26, in which Confucius complains of the prevalence of various types of "masquerading."
37. If one were to object that there is no notion of sin in Confucianism, my response is that the phenomenon that Royce labels "sin" in *The World and the Individual*, the deliberate inattention to a moral obligation, is indeed present in Confucianism.

38. Here I draw largely on the summaries of these theories provided by Linda Radzik in *Making Amends*.
39. Radzik, *Making Amends*, 46.
40. Royce, *The Problem of Christianity*, 168.
41. Ibid., 157.
42. Ibid., 168.
43. Ibid., 158.
44. Ibid., 174–175.
45. Ibid., 169 (emphasis in original).
46. Ibid., 176.
47. Ibid., 179.
48. Ibid., 169–170.
49. Ibid., 176.
50. Ibid., 178.
51. Ibid., 176.
52. Ibid., 178.
53. Ibid., 176.
54. Ibid., 160.
55. Ibid., 180.
56. Ibid. (emphasis in original).
57. Ibid.
58. Ibid., 181.
59. Ibid., 178.
60. Some of the content of this section repeats some of the content in my "Confess Your Contradictions: Schelling, Royce, and the Art of Atonement," *Journal of Speculative Philosophy* 26, no. 3 (2012): 516–530.
61. Another resemblance is noteworthy. As Heiner Roetz points out, expressions such as *xue chi* 雪恥 ("wash off" shame) imply that shame is an impurity to be cleansed. The same sort of metaphor is present in Royce's discussion (e.g., "Forgiveness does not wash out a word of the record that the moving finger of treason has written." [Royce, *The Problem of Christianity*, 178]). See Heiner Roetz, *Confucian Ethics of the Axial Age: A Reconstruction under the Aspect of the Breakthrough Toward Postconventional Thinking* (Albany: State University of New York Press, 1993), 177.

62. A future discussion would take up the *Mencius* in more detail. I am particularly struck by passages such as 1A5, which I quote in part: "King Hui of Liang said, 'Under Heaven there was no state stronger than Jin, as you, venerable sir, are aware. But when it came to my reign, Jin was defeated by Qi in the east, and my oldest son died there. In the west seven hundred *li* were lost to Qin, while in the south we were humiliated by Chu. Having incurred such shame, I wish, for the sake of the departed, to expunge it. How may this be done?'" The notion of expunging shame for the sake of the departed is highly rich in symbolism and meaning. It is a unique variety of atonement the likes of which I do not address in the present discussion.
63. Huang Kan, quoted in Slingerland, *Confucius Analects*, 228.
64. It is tempting to read the last lines of *Analects* 7.31 ("How fortunate I am! If I happen to make a mistake, others are sure to inform me.") as consistent with *Analects* 7.3, however, in the context of the passage, these words are laced with sarcasm.
65. See, for instance, *Analects* 17.1, in which Confucius waits for a time when Yang Huo would not be home to acknowledge his gift of a suckling pig; *Analects* 17.4, in which Confucius harshly criticizes the quality of music and singing that he overhears; *Analects* 17.20, in which Confucius feigns illness to avoid having a meeting with Ru Bei and plays music and sings, knowing that Ru Bei's messenger is within earshot.
66. *Analects* 17.1 and 17.4 both end with Confucius making up for his transgression in some fashion. *Analects* 17.20 does not, though it is also possible that Confucius does not actually transgress here but instead chooses a clever and stinging method to teach a lesson to Ru Bei about the ritual impropriety involved in his seeking a meeting with Confucius. For this interpretation, see Slingerland, *Confucius Analects*, 208–209.
67. I say "perhaps" because we do not know the chronology of these remarks from Confucius. It very well could be that a remark recorded in book 6 of the *Analects* preceded, in real time, a remark recorded in book 5.
68. See also *Mencius* 2A2 and 2A9.

69. Slingerland, *Confucius Analects*, 49.
70. There are several relevant passages in the *Analects* that corroborate this reading. Passages not yet considered in the present study include *Analects* 1.7, 12.21, and 14.25.
71. There are several relevant passages in the *Analects* that corroborate this reading. For an additional passage featuring a related exchange between Confucius and Ji Kangzi, see 2.20.
72. *Analects* 15.24: "Zigong asked, 'Is there one expression that can be acted upon until the end of one's days?' The Master replied, 'There is *shu*: do not impose on others what you yourself do not want.'"
73. Slingerland, *Confucius Analects*, 112 (emphasis in original). Slingerland flips from "Min Ziqian" to "Min Zijian," but I have preserved the former spelling throughout.
74. It must be admitted that counterfactuals like these are quite difficult, if not impossible, to establish. How could Royce (or anyone) know that a community is stronger in the aftermath of treason than it would have been had the treason never occurred? Examples such as the story of Min Ziqian bring into relief the difficulty of accepting this position.
75. Royce, *The Problem of Christianity*, 168.
76. In the *Han Feizi*, it is reported that this is what happened, and that Upright Gong was executed, but this telling of the story may be shaped by social-political motives of Han Feizi's own. As the story is told in the *Lüshi Chunqiu*, Upright Gong turns himself in, pleas to not be executed on account of his filiality for asking to be executed in place of his father, and asks who in the state would not deserve to be executed if someone of his filiality and honesty should be executed. The King of Chu then called off the execution. Confucius heard about this and said, "So weird is [Upright Gong's] way of being honest. He made a sacrifice with his own father in order to gain the repute [of honesty]. Indeed, the honesty of [Upright Gong] is no better than having no honesty." See Huaiyu Wang, "Piety and Individuality Through a Convoluted Path of Rightness: Exploring the Confucian Art of Moral Discretion via *Analects* 13.18," *Asian Philosophy* 21, no. 4 (2011): 397–398, 414–415n4.

77. It does seem that there would have been a threat of harm coming to both the father and son. The penalty for stealing a sheep would have been severe, perhaps even death (ibid., 398, 415n6).
78. See, for example, K. K. Yeo, *Musing with Confucius and Paul: Toward a Chinese Christian Theology* (Eugene: Cascade Books, 2008).

CONCLUSION

1. Smid, *Methodologies of Comparative Philosophy*.
2. See Joseph Grange, "The Disappearance of the Public Good: Confucius, Dewey, Rorty," *Philosophy East and West* 46, no. 3 (1996): 351–366, and Yong Huang (ed.), *Rorty, Pragmatism, and Confucianism* (Albany: State University of New York Press, 2009). Of the contributions in Huang's volume, two stand out for comparing Rorty with Mencius: Peimin Ni, "A Comparative Examination of Rorty's and Mencius's Theories of Human Nature" (101–115), and James Behuniak Jr., "Rorty and Mencius on Family, Nature, and Morality" (117–127).

Bibliography

Ames, Roger T., and David L. Hall. *Daodejing: A Philosophical Translation*. New York: Ballantine Books, 2003.

Ames, Roger T., and Henry Rosemont, Jr. *The Analects of Confucius: A Philosophical Translation*. New York: Ballantine Books, 1998.

Ames, Van Meter. *Zen and American Thought*. Honolulu: University of Hawaii Press, 1962.

Angle, Stephen C. *Sagehood: The Contemporary Significance of Neo-Confucianism*. New York: Oxford University Press, 2009.

"atonement, n." OED Online. September 2015. Oxford University Press. http://www.oed.com/view/Entry/12599?redirectedFrom=atonement. Accessed 27 September 2015.

Barrett, Nathaniel F. "A Confucian Theory of Shame." *Sophia* 54, no. 2 (2015): 143–163.

Behuniak, James, Jr. *Mencius on Becoming Human*. Albany: State University of New York Press, 2005.

———. "Rorty and Mencius on Family, Nature, and Morality." In *Rorty, Pragmatism, and Confucianism*, ed. Yong Huang, 117–127. Albany: State University of New York, 2009.

Berthrong, John. "From Xunzi to Boston Confucianism." *Journal of Chinese Philosophy* 30, nos. 3–4 (2003): 433–450.

Bloom, Irene. *Mencius*. New York: Columbia University Press, 2009.

Book of Common Prayer. http://www.bcponline.org/. Accessed 27 September 2015.

Cady, Lyman V. "Thoreau's Quotations from the Confucian Books in *Walden*." *American Literature* 33, no. 1 (1961): 20–32.

Cai, Degui. "Hawaiian Confucianism." *Journal of Chinese Philosophy* 32, no. 1 (2005): 123–138.

Carpenter, Frederic Ives. *Emerson and Asia*. Cambridge: Harvard University Press, 1931.

Chapman, John Jay. *Emerson, and Other Essays*. New York: AMS Press, 1965 [1899].

Chen, David T. Y. "Thoreau and Taoism." In *Asian Response to American Literature*, ed. C. D. Narasimhaiah, 406–416. New York: Barnes & Noble, 1972.

Cheng, Aimin. "Humanity as 'A Part and Parcel of Nature'": A Comparative Study of Thoreau's and Taoist Concepts of Nature." In *Thoreau's Sense of Place: Essays in American Environmental Writing*, ed. Richard J. Schneider, 207–220. Iowa City: University of Iowa Press, 2000.

Cheng, Chung-ying. "Preface." *Journal of Chinese Philosophy* 36, no. 1 (2009): 1–2.

Christy, Arthur. The Orient in American Transcendentalism: A Study of Emerson, Thoreau and Alcott. New York: Octagon Books, 1963 (1932).

Collie, David. *The Chinese Classical Work, Commonly Called the Four Books*. Malacca: The Mission Press, 1828.

Connolly, Tim. *Doing Philosophy Comparatively*. New York: Bloomsbury, 2015.

———. "Fallibilism in Early Confucian Philosophy." Peirce's Philosophy and Chinese Philosophy Session, Charles S. Peirce Centennial Congress. University of Massachusetts–Lowell, July 16, 2014 (unpublished paper).

———. "Friendship and Filial Piety: Relational Ethics in Aristotle and Early Confucianism." *Journal of Chinese Philosophy* 39, no. 1 (2012): 71–88.

Couplet, Philippe, and R. F. Incorcetta. *Confucius Sinarum Philosophus*. Paris: Apud Danielem Horthemels, 1687.

———. "The Morals of Confucius." In *The Phenix: A Collection of Old and Rare Fragments*. New York: W. Gowan, 1835.

Cua, A. S. "The Conceptual Aspect of Hsün-Tzu's Philosophy of Human Nature." *Philosophy East and West* 27, no. 4 (1977): 373–389.
———. "The Quasi-Empirical Aspect of Hsün-Tzu's Philosophy of Human Nature." *Philosophy East and West* 28, no. 1 (1978): 3–19.
Curti, Merle. *Human Nature in American Thought: A History*. Madison: University of Wisconsin Press, 1980.
Davis, Allen F. *American Heroine: The Life and Legend of Jane Addams*. New York: Oxford University Press, 1973.
Dolan, Neal, and Laura Jane Wey. "Emerson and China." In *A Power to Translate the World: New Essays on Emerson and International Culture*, ed. David LaRocca and Ricardo Miguel-Alfonso, 236–248. Lebanon: University Press of New England, 2015.
Dooley, Patrick K. "Thoreau on Civil Disobedience: From Pacifism to Violence." *Journal of Thought* 13, no. 3 (1978):180–187.
Eberhard, Wolfram. *Guilt and Sin in Traditional China*. Berkeley and Los Angeles: University of California Press, 1967.
Elstein, David. "Why Early Confucianism Cannot Generate Democracy." *Dao: A Journal of Comparative Philosophy* 9, no. 4 (2010): 427–443.
Emerson, John. "Thoreau's Construction of Taoism." *Thoreau Journal Quarterly* 12, no. 2 (1980): 5–9.
Emerson, Ralph Waldo. "Friendship." In *Essays & Poems*, ed. Joel Porte, Harold Bloom, and Paul Kane, 339–354. New York: Library of America, 1996.
———. *Journals and Miscellaneous Notebooks of Ralph Waldo Emerson*, Vol. II: 1822–1826, ed. William H. Gilman, Alfred R. Ferguson, and Merrell R. Davis. Cambridge: Belknap Press, 1961.
———. *Journals and Miscellaneous Notebooks of Ralph Waldo Emerson*, Vol. V: 1835–1838, ed. Merton M. Sealts. Cambridge: Belknap Press, 1965.
———. *Journals and Miscellaneous Notebooks of Ralph Waldo Emerson*, Vol. VI: 1824–1838, edited by Ralph H. Orth. Cambridge, MA: Belknap Press, 1966.
———. *Journals and Miscellaneous Notebooks of Ralph Waldo Emerson*. Vol. VIII: 1841–1848, ed. William H. Gilman and J. E. Parsons. Cambridge: Belknap Press, 1970.

---. *Journals and Miscellaneous Notebooks of Ralph Waldo Emerson*, Vol. XIII: 1852–1855, ed. Ralph H. Orth and Alfred R. Ferguson. Cambridge: Belknap Press, 1977.

---. *Journals and Miscellaneous Notebooks of Ralph Waldo Emerson*, Vol. XV, ed. Linda Allardt, David W. Hill, and Ruth H. Bennett. Cambridge: Belknap Press, 1982.

---. *Representative Men and Miscellanies*. Boston and New York: Houghton Mifflin Company, 1921.

---. "Society." In *The Early Lectures of Ralph Waldo Emerson*, Vol. II, ed. Stephen E. Whicher, Robert E. Spiller, and Wallace E. Williams, 98–112. Cambridge: Belknap Press, 1964.

"Ethnical Scriptures." In *The Dial: A Magazine for Literature, Philosophy, and Religion*, Vol. III. New York: Russell & Russell, 1961 (April 1843).

---. In *The Dial: A Magazine for Literature, Philosophy, and Religion*, Vol. IV. New York: Russell & Russell, 1961 (October 1843).

Fields, Rick. How the Swans Came to the Lake: A Narrative History of Buddhism in America. Boston: Shambhala, 1992.

Fingarette, Herbert. "How the *Analects* Portrays the Ideal of Efficacious Authority." *Journal of Chinese Philosophy* 8, no. 1 (1981): 29–50.

Foust, Mathew A. "Confess Your Contradictions: Schelling, Royce, and the Art of Atonement." *Journal of Speculative Philosophy* 26, no. 3 (2012): 516–530.

---. "Confucianism and American Pragmatism." *Philosophy Compass* 10, no. 6 (2015): 369–378.

---. "Confucius and Emerson on the Virtue of Self-Reliance." In *A Power to Translate the World: New Essays on Emerson and International Culture*, ed. David LaRocca and Ricardo Miguel-Alfonso, 249–261. Lebanon: University Press of New England, 2015.

---. "Introduction: Chinese and American Philosophies: Broadening a Comparative Horizon." *Journal of Chinese Philosophy* 39, no. 2 (2012): 169–173.

---. "Loyalty in the Teachings of Confucius and Josiah Royce." *Journal of Chinese Philosophy* 39, no. 2 (2012): 192–206.

---. "Nitobe and Royce: Bushidō and the Philosophy of Loyalty." *Philosophy East and West* 65, no. 4 (2015): 1174–1193.

———. "Perplexities of Filiality: Confucius and Jane Addams on the Private/Public Distinction." *Asian Philosophy* 18, no. 2 (2008): 149–166.

———. "Tragedy and the Sorrow of Finitude: Reflections on Sin and Death in the Philosophy of Josiah Royce." *The Pluralist* 2, no. 2 (2007): 106–114.

Fung, Yu-lan. *A History of Chinese Philosophy*, Vol. 1. Princeton: Princeton University Press, 1952 (1934).

Fuss, Peter. *The Moral Philosophy of Josiah Royce*. Cambridge: Harvard University Press, 1965.

Geaney, Jane. "Guarding Moral Boundaries: Shame in Early Confucianism." *Philosophy East and West* 54, no. 2 (2004): 113–142.

Gentz, Joachim. "Confucius Confronting Contingency in the *Lunyu* and the *Gongyang Zhuan*." *Journal of Chinese Philosophy* 39, no. 1 (2012): 60–70.

Goldberg, Philip. *American Veda: From Emerson and the Beatles to Yoga and Meditation—How Indian Spirituality Changed the West*. New York: Harmony Books, 2013.

Goldin, Paul Rakita. *Rituals of the Way: The Philosophy of Xunzi*. Chicago and La Salle: Open Court, 1999.

———. "Xunzi's Piety." In *Confucian Spirituality*, Vol. 1, ed. Tu Weiming and Mary Evelyn Tucker, 287–303. New York: Crossroad, 2003.

Goodman, Russell B. "Emerson and Skepticism: A Reading of 'Friendship.'" *European Journal of Pragmatism and American Philosophy* 2, no. 2 (2010): 5–15.

Grange, Joseph. "The Disappearance of the Public Good: Confucius, Dewey, Rorty." *Philosophy East and West* 46, no. 3 (1996): 351–366.

———. *John Dewey, Confucius, and Global Philosophy*. Albany: State University of New York Press, 2004.

Grossman, Richard. *The Tao of Emerson: The Wisdom of the Tao Te Ching as Found in the Words of Ralph Waldo Emerson*. New York: The Modern Library, 2007.

Haack, Susan. "Do Not Block the Way of Inquiry." *Transactions of the Charles S. Peirce Society* 50, no. 3 (2014): 319–339.

Hall, David L., and Roger T. Ames. *Daodejing: A Philosophical Translation*. New York: Ballantine Books, 2003.

———. *The Democracy of the Dead: Dewey, Confucius, and the Hope for Democracy in China*. Chicago and La Salle: Open Court, 1999.

———. *Thinking from the Han: Self, Truth, and Transcendence in Chinese and Western Culture*. Albany: State University of New York Press, 1998.

———. *Thinking Through Confucius*. Albany: State University of New York Press, 1987.

Harrison, John S. *The Teachers of Emerson*. New York: Sturgis & Walton, 1910.

Hocking, William Ernest. "Chu Hsi's Theory of Knowledge." *Harvard Journal of Asiatic Studies* 1, no. 1 (1936): 109–127.

———. *Re-Thinking Missions: A Layman's Inquiry after One Hundred Years*. Laymen's Foreign Missions Inquiry Commission of Appraisal, William Ernest Hocking, chairman. New York: Harper and Brothers, 1932.

Hodder, Alan D. *Thoreau's Ecstatic Witness*. New Haven: Yale University Press, 2001.

Holt, Linda Brown. "Chinese Philosophy in America: How It Influenced Henry Thoreau." http://thoreau.eserver.org/Chinese.html. Accessed 27 September 2015.

Huang, Yong, ed. *Rorty, Pragmatism, and Confucianism*. Albany: State University of New York Press, 2009.

Inada, Kenneth K., and Nolan P. Jacobson, eds. *Buddhism and American Thinkers*. Albany: State University of New York Press, 1984.

Jackson, Carl T. *The Oriental Religions and American Thought: Nineteenth-Century Explorations*. Westport: Greenwood Press, 1981.

James, William. *Talks to Teachers on Psychology and to Students on Some of Life's Ideals*. New York: Henry Holt and Company, 1904 (1899).

———. *The Varieties of Religious Experience*. London and New York: Routledge, 2002 (1902).

———. *The Will to Believe and Other Essays in Popular Philosophy*. New York: Dover, 1956 (1897).

———. *The Works of William James: Essays in Religion and Morality*. Ed. Frederick Burkhardt and Fredson Bowers. Cambridge: Harvard University Press, 1982.

Jiang, Yi, and Binmin Zhong. "Peirce Studies in China in the 21st Century." *European Journal of Pragmatism and American Philosophy* 6, no. 2 (2014): 252–260.

Kaag, John. "Peirce and Plato on the Fixation of Belief." *Transactions of the Charles S. Peirce Society* 48, no. 4 (2012): 512–529.

Kasser, Jeff. "How Settled Are Settled Beliefs in 'The Fixation of Belief'?" *Transactions of the Charles S. Peirce Society* 47, no. 2 (2011): 226–247.

Lai, Whalen. "Friendship in Confucian China: Classical and Late Ming." In *Friendship East and West: Philosophical Perspectives*, ed. Oliver Leaman, 215–250. Surrey: Curzon, 1995.

Legge, James. *Confucian Analects, the Great Learning, and the Doctrine of the Mean*. The Chinese Classics I. London: Trübner, 1861.

Lekan, Todd. "Appreciating the Impersonal in Emerson (That's What Friends Are For)." *Journal of Speculative Philosophy* 21, no. 2 (2007): 91–105.

Li, Chenyang. *The Confucian Philosophy of Harmony*. New York: Routledge, 2014.

Lu, Xiufen. "Rethinking Confucian Friendship." *Asian Philosophy* 20, no. 3 (2010): 225–245.

Madden, Edward H., and Peter H. Hare. "Reflections on Civil Disobedience." *Journal of Value Inquiry* 4, no. 2 (1970): 81–95.

Marshman, Joshua. *The Works of Confucius: Containing the Original Text with a Translation*. Serampore: Mission Press, 1809.

Mullis, Eric C. "Confucius and Aristotle on the Goods of Friendship." *Dao: A Journal of Comparative Philosophy* 9, no. 4 (2010): 391–405.

Munro, Donald J. *The Concept of Man in Early China*. Stanford: Stanford University Press, 1969.

Murthy, Viren. "The Democratic Potential of Confucian *Minben* Thought." *Asian Philosophy* 10, no. 1 (2000): 33–47.

Neville, Robert Cummings. *Boston Confucianism: Portable Tradition in the Late-Modern World*. Albany: State University of New York Press, 2000.

———. "Confucianism as a World Philosophy." *Journal of Chinese Philosophy* 21, no. 1 (1994): 5–25.

———. "Metaphysics and World Philosophy: W. E. Hocking on

Chinese Philosophy." In *A William Ernest Hocking Reader*, ed. John Lachs and D. Micah Hester, 367–382. Nashville: Vanderbilt University Press, 2004.

———. *The Highroad Around Modernism*. Albany: State University of New York Press, 1992.

Newfield, Christopher J. "Loving Bondage: Emerson's Ideal Relationships." *ATQ* 5, no. 3 (1991): 183–193.

Ni, Peimin. "A Comparative Examination of Rorty's and Mencius's Theories of Human Nature." In *Rorty, Pragmatism, and Confucianism*, ed. Yong Huang, 101–115. Albany: State University of New York Press, 2009.

Nitobe, Inazo. *Bushido: The Soul of Japan*. New York: Dover, 2004 (1900).

Odin, Steve. *The Social Self in Zen and American Pragmatism*. Albany: State University of New York Press, 1996.

Oliver, Egbert S. "The Asia in Emerson's Mind." *Korean Survey* 2 (1953): 10–12.

Parker, Kelly A. "Atonement and Eidetic Extinction." In *Josiah Royce for the Twenty-First Century*, ed. Kelly A. Parker and Krzysztof Piotr Skowronski, 213–223. Lanham: Lexington Books, 2012.

Pauthier, Jean-Pierre Guillaume. *Confucius et Mencius: Les Quatres Livres de Philosophie Morale et Politique de la Chine*. Paris: Charpentier, 1840.

———. *Les Livres Sacrés de l'Orient*. Paris: Société du Panthéon Littéraire, 1841.

Peirce, Charles S. "The Fixation of Belief." In *Charles S. Peirce: Selected Writings (Values in a Universe of Chance)*, ed. Philip P. Wiener, 91–112. New York: Dover, 1958.

———. "The Fixation of Belief." In *Charles S. Peirce: Illustrations of the Logic of Science*, ed. Cornelis de Waal, 43–78. Chicago: Open Court, 2014.

Radzik, Linda. *Making Amends: Atonement in Morality, Law and Politics*. Oxford: Oxford University Press, 2011.

Riepe, Dale. *The Philosophy of India and Its Influence on American Thought*. Springfield: Thomas Press, 1970.

Roetz, Heiner. *Confucian Ethics of the Axial Age: A Reconstruction under the Aspect of the Breakthrough Toward Postconventional Thinking.* Albany: State University of New York Press, 1993.

Rothenberg, Paula S. "Peirce's Defense of the Scientific Method." *Journal of the History of Philosophy* 13, no. 4 (1975): 481–490.

Royce, Josiah. *The Conception of God.* Bristol: Thoemmes Press, 2000 (1897).

———. *The Philosophy of Loyalty.* Nashville: Vanderbilt University Press, 1995 (1908).

———. *The Problem of Christianity.* Washington, DC: Catholic University of America Press, 2001 (1913).

———. *The Sources of Religious Insight.* New York: Charles Scribner's Sons, 1912.

———. *Studies of Good and Evil.* New York: D. Appleton and Company, 1902 (1898).

———. *The World and the Individual.* Second Series. New York: Dover, 1959 (1901).

Rusk, Ralph L. *The Letters of Ralph Waldo Emerson.* New York: Columbia University Press, 1939.

Sattelmeyer, Robert. *Thoreau's Reading: A Study in Intellectual History.* Princeton: Princeton University Press, 1988.

Scott, David. "Rewalking Thoreau and Asia: 'Light from the East' for 'A Very Yankee Sort of Oriental.'" *Philosophy East & West* 57, no. 1 (2007): 14–39.

Sebouhian, George. "A Dialogue with Death: An Examination of Emerson's 'Friendship.'" *Studies in the American Renaissance* (1989): 219–239.

Seok, Bongrae. "Moral Psychology of Shame in Early Confucian Philosophy." *Frontiers of Philosophy in China* 10, no. 1 (2015): 21–57.

Shen, Russell. "Dissimilarities between Deweyan Pragmatism and Confucianism." *Paideusis* 20, no. 1 (2012): 24–32.

Short, T. L. "Peirce on the Aim of Inquiry: Another Reading of 'Fixation.'" *Transactions of the Charles S. Peirce Society* 36, no. 1 (2000): 1–23.

Shusterman, Richard. "Pragmatism and East-Asian Thought." *Metaphilosophy* 35, nos. 1–2 (2004): 13–43.

Sim, May. "Dewey and Confucius: On Moral Education." *Journal of Chinese Philosophy* 36, no. 1 (2009): 85–105.

Simmons, Kyle Bryant. "Emerson, the American Confucius: An Exploration of Confucian Motifs in the Early Writings (1830–1843) of Ralph Waldo Emerson." PhD Dissertation. The University of Texas at Dallas, 2013.

Simon, Gary. "What Henry David Thoreau Didn't Know about Lao Tzu: Taoist Parallels in Thoreau." *Literature East and West* 16 (1973): 253–271.

Singer, Peter. *Democracy and Disobedience*. Oxford: Clarendon Press, 1973.

Slingerland, Edward. *Confucius Analects: With Selections from Traditional Commentaries*. Indianapolis: Hackett, 2003.

Smid, Robert W. *Methodologies of Comparative Philosophy: The Pragmatist and Process Traditions*. Albany: State University of New York Press, 2009.

Stephens, Daniel J. "Confucianism, Pragmatism, and Socially Beneficial Philosophy." *Journal of Chinese Philosophy* 36, no. 1 (2009): 53–67.

Takanashi, Yoshio. *Emerson and Neo-Confucianism: Crossing Paths over the Pacific*. New York: Palgrave Macmillan, 2014.

Tan, Hongbo. "Confucius at Walden Pond: Thoreau's Unpublished Confucian Translations." In *Studies in the American Renaissance*, ed. Joel Myerson, 275–303. Charlottesville: University Press of Virginia, 1993.

Tan, Sor-hoon. "Authoritative Master Kong (Confucius) in an Authoritarian Age." *Dao: A Journal of Comparative Philosophy* 9, no. 2 (2010): 137–149.

———. "China's Pragmatist Experiment in Democracy: Hu Shih's Pragmatism and Dewey's Influence in China." *Metaphilosophy* 35, nos. 1–2 (2004): 44–64.

———. *Confucian Democracy: A Deweyan Reconstruction*. Albany: State University of New York Press, 2004.

———. "Mentor or Friend? Confucius and Aristotle on Equality and Ethical Development in Friendship." *International Studies in Philosophy* 33, no. 4 (2001): 99–121.

Thoreau, Henry David. *Civil Disobedience, Solitude and Life Without Principle.* Amherst: Prometheus Books, 1998 (1849).

———. *Walden; or, Life in the Woods.* New York: Dover, 1995 (1854).

Tiwald, Justin. "A Right of Rebellion in the *Mengzi*?" *Dao: A Journal of Comparative Philosophy* 7, no. 3 (2008): 269–282.

Tu, Jiliang L., ed. *The Selected Writings of C. S. Peirce.* Beijing: Publishing House of China's Social Sciences, 2006.

Van Norden, Bryan W. "Mengzi and Xunzi: Two Views of Human Agency." *International Philosophical Quarterly* 32, no. 2 (1992): 161–184.

Versluis, Arthur. *American Gurus: From Transcendentalism to New Age Religion.* New York: Oxford University Press, 2014.

Walker, Margaret Urban. *Moral Repair: Reconstructing Moral Relations after Wrongdoing.* Cambridge: Cambridge University Press, 2006.

Wang, Huaiyu. "Piety and Individuality Through a Convoluted Path of Rightness: Exploring the Confucian Art of Moral Discretion via *Analects* 13.18." *Asian Philosophy* 21, no. 4 (2011): 395–418.

Wang, Jessica Ching-sze. *John Dewey in China: To Teach and to Learn.* Albany: State University of New York Press, 2010.

Watson, Burton. *Xunzi: Basic Writings.* New York: Columbia University Press, 2003.

Wen, Haiming. *Confucian Pragmatism as the Art of Contextualizing Personal Experience and World.* Lanham: Lexington Books, 2009.

Wong, David B. "Xunzi on Moral Motivation." In *Chinese Language, Thought, and Culture: Nivison and His Critics*, ed. Philip J. Ivanhoe, 202–223. Chicago and La Salle: Open Court, 1996.

Yearley, Lee H. "Virtues and Religious Virtues in the Confucian Tradition." In *Confucian Spirituality*, Volume One, ed. Tu Weiming and Mary Evelyn Tucker, 134–162. New York: Crossroad, 2003.

Yeo, K. K. *Musing with Confucius and Paul: Toward a Chinese Christian Theology.* Eugene: Cascade Books, 2008.

Yutang, Lin. *The Wisdom of America*. New York: The John Day Company, 1950.

———. *The Wisdom of India and China*. New York: The Modern Library, 1942.

Zhang Shanruo Ning. *Confucianism in Contemporary Chinese Politics: An Actionable Account of Authoritarian Political Culture*. Lanham: Lexington Books, 2016.

Index

Addams, Jane, 7, 155n27
American Pragmatism, 7, 8–12
American Transcendentalism, 7, 10, 12, 14, 15–17, 132
Aristotle, 27
atonement, 103–104, 113–126
authority, 49, 53, 61–62, 81, 150n58, 152n41

Bo Yi, 120–121, 124
Boston Confucianism, 11–12
Buddhism, 6, 11, 102
Bushido, 102

chi 道. *See* shame
China, 6, 16, 102, 103, 136n14
Christianity, 11, 12, 101, 104, 116, 126–127, 157n11
civil disobedience
 defined, 44–45
 (essay, see Thoreau, Henry David, "Civil Disobedience")
Collie, David, 19, 140n5, 140n7, 140n8
comparative philosophy, 1–5, 10–12, 129–131, 131–133 (also see "world philosophy")
Confucius, 6, 7–10, 14, 15, 16, 17, 25–32, 39–40, 41–44, 59, 61–62, 63–64, 69–79, 80–81, 83, 101, 102, 108–112, 116–127, 129, 130, 131
conscience, 45, 49–50

Daxue. See *The Great Learning*
dao 道 (way, path), 6, 29–30, 32, 56, 58, 64, 69, 70, 71, 73, 74, 77, 80, 108, 109, 110, 112, 118, 121, 123, 143n40, 147n14
Daodejing, 147n23
Daoism, 6, 11, 145n1, 154n11
de 德. *See* virtue
Dewey, John, 5, 7–10, 129
The Dial, 19, 21, 42
The Doctrine of the Mean. See *Zhongyong*

Emerson, Ralph Waldo, 5, 7, 14–15, 19–40, 42, 129, 130

Essays: First Series, 32
"Friendship," 22, 32–39, 40
Journals, 19, 21
"Society," 21–24, 32, 33, 34, 40
"Speech at Banquet in Honor of Chinese Embassy," 19–20
empathy. See *shu*

filiality. See *xiao*
forgiveness, 101, 114, 121, 124–125, 160n61
friendship, 19–40, 133
(essay, see Emerson, Ralph Waldo, "Friendship")
Fuller, Margaret, 140n5

God, 23, 34, 36, 102, 103, 107, 156n35
Goodman, Nelson, 132
The Great Learning (*Daxue*), 19, 132
guilt, 102–107

Han Feizi, 162n76
harmony. See *he*
he 和 (harmony), 78–79, 95, 109–110, 112
Hinduism, 6
Hocking, William Ernest, 132, 136n14
Hu Shih, 7–8
human nature, 83–100

India, 102, 136n14
inquiry, 61–81

James, William, 7, 15, 16, 84, 92–100, 129, 130, 132
A Pluralistic Universe, 93
Principles of Psychology, 84
Talks to Teachers on Psychology and to Students on Some of Life's Ideals, 84
"The Moral Equivalent of War," 96
"The Moral Philosopher and the Moral Life," 98
"The Sentiment of Rationality," 93
The Varieties of Religious Experience, 84, 93
The Will to Believe and Other Essays in Popular Philosophy, 84
Japan, 7, 102, 136n14
Jesus, 20
junzi 君子 (exemplary person, authoritative person), 25, 29, 50, 52, 72–73, 75, 79–80, 89, 111–112, 117–118, 122, 142n28, 149n44

learning. See *xue*
Legge, James, 19, 140n8
li 禮 (ritual, rites, ritual propriety), 46, 50–51, 61, 71–72, 76, 88, 90–92, 99, 110, 121, 149n45, 154n14, 161n66
Lin Yutang, 21

Marshman, Joshua, 19, 21, 22
Master Zeng, 29, 31
Mead, George Herbert, 7
Mencius, 6, 14, 15, 16, 17, 20, 42–44, 52–53, 56–57, 58, 60, 83–84, 84–87, 88, 89, 91–92, 93–95, 97–100, 101, 102, 108–112, 121, 126, 130, 131, 132–133
Min Ziqian, 124–125

minben 民本 ("people as root"), 53, 57

Neo-Confucianism, 11, 132, 141n11
Neo-Pragmatism, 132
Nitobe, Inazo, 102
Northrop, F.S.C., 132

Odes. See *Shijing*

Pauthier, Jean-Pierre Guillaume, 42
Peirce, Charles, 7, 15, 16, 62–68, 69, 70, 75, 76, 79–81, 129, 131
    "The Fixation of Belief," 62–68
Platonism, 11
Pragmatism. *See* American Pragmatism
Putnam, Hilary, 132

Quine, W.V.O., 132

reciprocity. See *shu*
reconciliation, 114–116, 123, 125–126
rectification of names. See *zhengming*
ren 仁 (humaneness, benevolence, Goodness) 13–14, 28–29, 31, 56, 59, 64, 73–74, 80, 112, 118–119, 123, 149n45
ritual. See *li*
Rorty, Richard, 132
Royce, Josiah, 7, 15, 17, 101–102, 104–107, 113–116, 126–127, 129
    Studies of Good and Evil, 158n14
    The Conception of God, 102, 105

The Philosophy of Loyalty, 102
The Problem of Christianity, 102, 113, 157n11
The Sources of Religious Insight, 102, 105–106
The World and the Individual, 102, 106–107, 114

Santayana, George, 132
shame, 43, 46–47, 102–107, 114, 125–126
    in Confucianism (*chi* 道), 43, 46, 52, 85, 86, 103, 108–112, 118, 121–122, 125–126, 147n14, 159n28, 159n30, 159n31
Shijing (*Odes*), 71, 132
Shintoism (Shinto) 102
shu 恕 (empathy, reciprocity), 123, 162n72
Shu Qi, 120–121, 124
sin, 103, 106–107, 115–116, 125
Singer, Peter, 49–50
study. See *xue*

Taoism. *See* Daoism
Thoreau, Henry David, 7, 14–15, 19, 41–52, 58–60, 129, 130
    A Week on the Concord and Merrimack Rivers, 42
    "Civil Disobedience," 42–43, 45–52, 58–59
    Letters, 42
    Walden, 41, 42, 46
    "Walking," 42
tian 天, 56, 63, 83, 132, 138n39
Transcendentalism. *See* American Transcendentalism

"Upright Gong," 125–126, 162n76

virtue, 22, 26–30, 36–39, 40, 46–48, 96, 101, 102
  in Confucianism (*de* 德), 46, 117, 119, 121, 122, 142n22, 148n28

Wang Yangming, 132
Whitehead, Alfred North, 5
world philosophy, 5–6. *Also see* "comparative philosophy"

xiao 孝 (filiality, filial piety), 59, 122–123, 124–126
xiaoren 小人 (petty person), 75, 79, 117–118, 122
xing 性 (natural disposition, natural tendencies) 83–94
xue 學 (learning, study), 22, 25, 29, 30–32, 38, 63–64, 70, 73, 79, 132

Xunzi, 7, 14, 16, 83–84, 84–85, 87–92, 93–95, 97–99, 130

Yan Hui, 73–74, 78, 119–120, 152n44, 159n28
yi 義 (rightness, dutifulness, appropriateness), 50–51, 56, 64, 85–86, 100, 112

Zen Buddhism, 6
Zengzi. *See* Master Zeng
zhengming 正名 ("rectification of names"), 51, 56–57
zhi 智 (wisdom, knowing), 85–87, 112, 132
Zhongyong (*The Doctrine of the Mean*), 19, 132
Zhu Xi, 121, 132, 136n14

www.ingramcontent.com/pod-product-compliance
Ingram Content Group UK Ltd.
Pitfield, Milton Keynes, MK11 3LW, UK
UKHW042013140426
5217IPUK00015B/1138